CASUALTY FIGURES

CASUALTY FIGURES

HOW FIVE MEN SURVIVED
THE FIRST WORLD WAR

Michèle Barrett

VERSO

London • New York

First published by Verso 2007
© Michèle Barrett 2007
All rights reserved

1 3 5 7 9 10 8 6 4 2

Verso
UK: 6 Meard Street, London W1F 0EG
USA: 180 Varick Street, New York, NY 10014-4606
www.versobooks.com

Verso is the imprint of New Left Books

ISBN-13: 978-1-84467-230-1

British Library Cataloguing in Publication Data
A catalogue record for this book is available from the British Library

Library of Congress Cataloging-in-Publication Data
A catalog record for this book is available from the Library of Congress

Typeset in Bembo by Hewer Text UK Ltd, Edinburgh
Printed in the USA by Maple Vail

Contents

Preface   xi

Introduction   1
Lieutenant John Willis Brown   34
Captain Douglas Darling   53
Bombardier Ronald Skirth   66
Air Vice-Marshal Sir William Tyrrell   92
Captain Lawrence Gameson   122

Afterword   153
Notes   159
Sources and further reading   163
Acknowledgements   165
Index   167

For
Linda King and Gilly Furse, Robin Barrett and
Michael Barrett, and with thanks to Helen Hudson.

Figures

1. Charles Sims, *I am the Abyss and I am Light* (1928).
2. William Orpen, *A Death Among the Wounded in the Snow* (1917–1918).
3. William Orpen, *The Mad Woman of Douai* (1918).
4. Paul Nash, *Void* (1918).

Preface

Shell-shock. How many a brief bombardment had its long-delayed after-effect in the minds of these survivors, many of whom had looked at their companions and laughed while inferno did its best to destroy them. Not then was their evil hour, but now . . .

Siegfried Sassoon, 1936[1]

The shell shock of the First World War has changed the way people think about the psychology of fighting. Many soldiers brought an end, even if a temporary one, to their ordeal when they developed physical symptoms which meant that they couldn't function. They literally couldn't walk, or talk − their legs were paralysed, their mouths mute. We can now, nearly ninety years on, recognize these 'hysterical' illnesses as forms of battle fatigue or post-traumatic stress. During the war itself, shell shock was an issue for military discipline and morale: a few soldiers were shot for cowardice or desertion, and many others were accused of malingering, and 'treated' accordingly.

But the end of the war did not bring the end of these psychological problems. If psychiatric military pensions are anything to go by, the mental fallout of the war carried on growing during the 1920s. There are scarcely any scientific studies of what happened to these men later, except for a group of shell-shocked American soldiers who were followed up in the mid 1920s: seven

years after the war less than 40 per cent were regarded as
functioning normally, and nearly 20 per cent were found to
be a burden to society.[2]

Casualty Figures describes the ways in which the psychological
damage of their First World War experiences affected the lives of
five particular men – these three soldiers and two military doctors
either had shell shock or treated it (or both). But their life stories
to me seemed to open up questions beyond shell shock, and to
help us reflect on wider aspects of the psychological consequences of war. I came to feel that shell shock, which has been
extensively studied by historians in terms of its causes, diagnosis,
treatment and interpretation, is frequently isolated from its
broader human implications. So I tell these men's stories in such
a way as to bring out the connections between 'shell shock' and
other mental consequences of their war experiences – which
include depression, exhaustion, bitterness, alcoholism, chronic
illness, self-destructive behaviour, unexplained or ambiguous
early death and failings as parents and partners.

This book, then, is a biography of five men. Their stories came
alive for me through the personal papers – diaries, letters,
memoirs, photograph albums – in the collections deposited at
the Imperial War Museum in London, and *Casualty Figures* is
based on these sources. But we need to read these personal
documents in the context of the war itself, and some of this I
have filled in from official unit diaries, regimental histories and
other military and historical sources.

I chose to write a multiple biography not because the bio-
graphies of individuals have some necessary guarantee of authen-
ticity – they obviously don't. But the device of concentrating on
one individual's experience provided a structure that allowed me
to resist the urge to generalization that is so common when
historians tackle this subject. From this distance of time it is easy
to be sympathetic to the men's suffering, or cynical about their
patriotism (or vice versa), without really engaging with the

circumstances in which shell shock developed. We need a deep and fine apprehension of what Raymond Williams called the 'structures of feeling' available to these men, in their lifetimes.[2] This is partly why the fiction and poetry of shell shock, from the war poets to Pat Barker, have struck a resonant chord with the reading public.

Although these are individual life stories, they are not about 'memory'. Much of the emotion that attaches to war stories, as indeed it does also to family history, is often thought of (wrongly, I think) in terms of memory. Personal memory is not what is important here. Nor do I believe that cultures can have 'memories', in any meaningful sense: societies can construct public memorials and organize ceremonies, and they can decide what is taught in history lessons. But the significant context of these life stories is not what can be *remembered* now: it is what has survived for us to study.

In the British case, social class is a relentless determinant of what kind of materials have survived. Staying at the home of some friends in the country while writing this book, I predicted quite confidently that someone in that large family would have died in the 1914–18 war, and that there would be a record of it. It took all of four minutes to find it on the bookshelves: a volume of privately printed letters and papers, assembled by his sister, for his sons to know him by. The collections in the War Museum, unusually wide-ranging by social class as they undoubtedly are, also reflect an unevenness in whose stories are there to be told. The materials for an understanding of the mental damage of the First World War are radically shaped by social and political factors, as I discuss at the end of the book.

Introduction

These are the stories of five men who experienced some of the worst conditions of the First World War, on the western front and at Gallipoli. Three of them were soldiers, two of them army doctors. These men, lucky enough not even to be seriously wounded, were among the unscathed survivors of the war that killed at least nine million. But they were not immune to the psychological damage of the war. For these five there were moments of terror, nauseating sights and smells, and temporary breakdowns. Some were classified, for a while, as 'shell-shocked'. This was nothing out of the ordinary. These five men were not among the dead in the casualty lists in the newspapers, but they were among the dead in a different way. In their own accounts of these experiences they were literally among the dead, as they coped with the gruesome aftermath of battles that left them living with corpses for company. How did they come to terms with these experiences? Did they become casualties too? Did they cope mentally as well as they did physically? How did they fare in the rest of their lives? How did they manage, as sons, husbands and fathers, when they returned from these extreme experiences?

Willis Brown was underage when he first tried to enlist. The son of a steel works manager in Sheffield, he was not happy at home. His father, bowing to the inevitable, got him into the engineering section of Winston Churchill's newly formed Royal

Naval Division. Willis was drafted to the Dardanelles campaign, to Gallipoli. As conditions worsened in the early summer of 1915, Willis was suffering from the dysentery endemic on the peninsula. Light-headed, he found himself alone in a trench full of dead Turks, and he gave up. He shovelled the bodies to one end of the trench then sat down at the other, apparently (he lost his memory) for several days. Given up for dead, he was eventually found, invalided out on a hospital ship and repatriated. It took him a long while to recover, if indeed he did. He took a commission in the Royal Field Artillery, but his military career during the war was dogged by illness, as was the rest of his life. It was only after his death that his sister Margaret, in a moving family memoir written in 1964, was able to explain to his disappointed son David why Willis had been so inadequate as a father. His health and life, she felt, had been wrecked by 'those horrible physical and psychological experiences in the first war'. The more he tried to bury them, she said, 'the more they ate into him'.

Douglas Darling, born in Aberdeen, was 28 years old and ranching 105 acres at Soda Creek, British Columbia, when he responded to the 1915 recruiting effort of the Canadian Overseas Expeditionary Force. By late 1916 he was in France, a lieutenant in the Canadian Machine Gun Corps. Darling was involved in the celebrated capture of Vimy Ridge by the Canadians in April 1917, and was awarded a Military Cross (MC) for his part in that action. For much of the battle he was in command of the 2nd Machine Gun Company of the Corps, playing a role in a barrage that was a landmark in military history. Douglas Darling had a strong conception of his duty, which he used to master his fear of the shelling, and what he called his 'nerves'. He believed that he had 'shell shock' in the months following Vimy. Throughout the war he wrote frequently to the woman who in early 1918 became his wife; his natural instinct for self-preservation became increasingly felt as a desire to survive in the hope of their future life together. That life was only to last six years after he was demobilized. In 1925, at the very young age of 38, Douglas Darling died. According to his daughter, the war had 'broken his health'. His son gave his papers to the Imperial War Museum, stating the family's view that he had died of the effects of shell shock.

Ronald Skirth started his army life as a corporal in the Royal Field Artillery. He quickly lost his corporal's stripe, and was demoted to bombardier, for refusing to use a French church as target practice – his journey towards becoming a pacifist had begun. In 1917 Ronald Skirth went through the battles of Messines and Third Ypres (Passchendaele). His accounts of both of them focus on the corpses he came across, on 'things' that were decomposing, and on the body of a young boy named 'Hans', whom he identified with. Skirth was then sent to the North Italian front. In Italy, he was treated in hospital for amnesia and shell shock. He also underwent a 'mystical religious experience', inspired by the war-renouncing St Martin. Vowing never again to take human life, Ronald Skirth set about his work as a layer of gun courses. He deliberately calculated the range of the guns to warn the opposing Austrians: 'our first rounds always fell wide or short', he said proudly. Recovered from his breakdown, Ron Skirth adopted the tactics of a Ghandi; he became a conscientious objector in the Artillery. Breathtaking in his rebellious attitude to military authority, Ron Skirth came to be a robust survivor in terms of his own sense of himself. In 1961, when he retired, he took his beloved wife Ella on a second honeymoon; they went to San Martino and the beautiful region of northern Italy where, he felt, his sanity had been redeemed.

William Tyrrell went to France in August 1914, aged 26, as the medical officer of the 2nd Battalion of the Lancashire Fusiliers. He was quickly decorated for bravery, winning one of the first MCs ever awarded, and he flourished as a regimental officer as well as a doctor. By the end of the war he held the rank of lieutenant colonel; after the war he joined the medical side of the RAF and rose to the rank of air vice-marshal. In late 1915, after more than a year at the front, Tyrrell's men were again slaughtered around him and he was buried alive. He broke down in tears at the sight of the battalion's riderless horses – the officers had all been killed. He was at first unable to control these tears, but after six months away from the front line he recovered, and was able to stay in post for the rest of the war. Tyrrell later said that he 'gave way to shell shock'. In June 1918 two of his brothers were killed – Alexander a hero of the Flying Corps, Marcus in a 'flying accident' which might have been suicide. William knew that Marcus had not been coping for some while; he had been trying to get his brother some leave. Tyrrell became the RAF's expert on fear, morale and courage, and was increasingly sure that his own breakdown had been caused by poor discipline. Outwardly successful, Sir William Tyrrell (Honorary Surgeon to the King) became an authoritarian, unhappily married, embittered and resentful man.

Lawrence Gameson was so keen to get into uniform that he got himself commissioned into the Royal Army Medical Corps on the very day that he graduated. On active service he was promoted to the rank of captain and decorated with the *Croix de Guerre*, but he still saw himself as a medical 'quasi-spectator' of the military action. Gameson was with a field ambulance at the Somme in 1916 and then for two years attached to an artillery regiment. His papers show his own struggle with the 'windiness' often thought to underlie breakdown in war. He was contemptuous of his own fear: 'I am disgusted to find that I cannot oust it', he wrote at one point. He did oust that fear, towards the end of the war. His war experience changed his life in another way, as he met his future wife, then an ambulance driver. Lawrence Gameson never intended his war diaries and memoir for publication: they contain frank clinical descriptions of sights that are usually wrapped up in euphemisms. His accounts of injuries are perhaps familiar; less so his calm and spare descriptions of necrosis in living tissue. Gameson devoted much of his time after the war to helping soldiers make claims for compensation. He had seen the conditions of the infantry, and knew how difficult it was to stay sane in them, and he was irritated at the attempt of the authorities to reduce their pension bills.

Most of these men, though not enjoying very good health, lived out a reasonably normal lifespan. Douglas Darling was the one who died very young. Looking at his death, in 1925, we can see the tug of family history and myth, the currents of feeling in which the lives of these men float. Darling's papers were given to the Imperial War Museum by his son George, towards the end of his own life. George Darling cited the cause of his father's premature death as the delayed effects of shell shock. If we call up Douglas Darling's death certificate, we find that he died at 37 West Hill, Dartford, Kent, on 1 December 1925. But the cause of death given there, by a Dr Renton, is listed as '1. Meningitis' and '2. Coma'. Were these words medical euphemisms for a death whose real causes – prolonged mental frailty resulting from his war experience – were too much of a stigma to be recorded? Or was the untimely but quite natural death of this man, who less than ten years before had been a fit young rancher in western Canada, so unbearable that the family laid the blame for it on the war?

Such questions bedevil the way we understand the fates of survivors of the First World War. There is often ambiguity in how early deaths were recorded. Alcoholism, of which many veterans died, was not a death for families to be proud of. Suicide, only decriminalized in Britain in 1961, was even worse. Euphemisms abounded. The painter Charles Sims had a son, a navy cadet aged only 16 years; the boy John was one of approximately 750 crew killed when HMS *Bulwark* accidentally blew up in Sheerness Harbour in November 1914. Charles Sims, who was a successful portrait painter and ran the training schools at the Royal Academy in London, became a war artist. He visited the western front and saw for himself the mass mutilation of the human body, whose perfection had been central to his own portrait painting. He could not paint damaged human figures. Instead, during the 1920s, he painted abstract mystical canvases in which perfect boyish forms figure prominently [see Fig. 1]. In 1928 Charles Sims committed suicide. His last paintings were described, somewhat disparagingly, by the Royal Academy as the product of a 'deranged mind'. Even though it was widely known that Sims had committed suicide – that he had put stones in his pockets and drowned himself – the word routinely used publicly to describe his mental illness was that he suffered from 'insomnia'. When Sims died, the obituaries emphasized the point that he had 'never recovered' from the death of his son, killed in action in the war. Another of his sons, Alan, later pointed to the mutilation of war and its affront to his aesthetic credo as the real cause of his death.

Death by suicide, and death from more passive forms of self-destruction such as alcoholism, can be difficult to distinguish. The stories we hear are the stories that the families repeat, the stories that make the most sense to them. These are often different from what is recorded on official documents such as death certificates. Several historians have quoted from the startling letters that the young Guy Nightingale wrote to his family from the Gallipoli campaign in 1915. Nightingale was a regular professional soldier, an officer (at that time a captain) in the Royal Munster Fusiliers, and he prided himself on being a lot tougher than the volunteers he worked along-side. His descriptions of the conditions at Gallipoli are hair-raising. Nightingale referred to the mountains of bodies as 'a grand sight', declared that he preferred killing Turks to taking them prisoner, boasted to his sister that Gallipoli was not as exciting as elephant hunting, and commented witheringly on men who aged rapidly and whose hair went white. Major Nightingale's regiment was disbanded in 1922. In 1935, on the twentieth anniversary of the Gallipoli landings, he shot himself.

Nightingale's story featured in *A Place Called Armageddon*, a book about the First World War.[1] A collection of his letters was printed, with an introduction by the book's editor. The account of Nightingale's death was based on an interview in the early 1970s with a surviving relative, his niece. The editor, Michael Moynihan, interpreted the suicide, the end of a 'road to despair', in the light of one particularly poignant and sad family photograph. Nightingale had been a lonely little boy, sent to school in England while his parents remained in India. He had never married, he had never replaced the family his regiment had been for him. He lived the life of a bachelor recluse, alone and drinking heavily. What does Nightingale's death certificate say? Certainly he died in April 1935, at his home, Thatch Cottage, Wedmore, Somerset, but there is no mention of shooting himself. The cause of death is given as '1a Cardiac Syncope [failure of the action of the heart]. b Delerium Tremens. c Chronic Alcoholism'. The death was registered by someone who lived at the same address, presumably a housekeeper. It was certified by a doctor in the usual manner, with no post-mortem required: would this doctor have been willing to perjure himself to protect the reputation of a lonely bachelor?

Two local papers, the *Wells Gazette* and the *Central Somerset Gazette*, gave accounts of Major Nightingale's funeral. We learn that far from being a recluse, 'he soon became popular' after he moved to the village of Wedmore in 1930, and that he was vice-captain of the local cricket club. The majority of the players at the club, along with 'a strong muster' from the British Legion, joined the family mourners at St Mary's Church.[2] Guy Nightingale was 43 years old. Curiously, only a week later the local papers featured the death of another war veteran. This story was of a man who had shot himself at his home. Nightingale's present next of kin, Elisabeth Coleman, his great-niece, confirmed to me that she understood from her mother 'that he did commit suicide and that this was a consequence, at least in part, of the trauma of his World War 1 experiences'. She went on to suggest, reasonably enough, that the reluctance to acknowledge publicly the nature of his death was, she assumed, related to feelings of guilt and also to the fact that 'suicide was a legal offence at that time and considered by some to disgrace both the victim and his or her family'. Of course this is right, and not only from the family's point of view. Would a doctor in 1935 have seen it that way? And if they were trying to protect his family, would the alcoholism have been cited? Is it possible that Nightingale simply drank himself to death, his heart failing coincidentally on the anniversary of the Gallipoli landings, rather than shooting himself? It may not be possible to answer those questions with certainty.

The untimely deaths of Douglas Darling, Charles Sims and Guy Nightingale have all been attributed to their wartime experiences. Whether they died by suicide, as was proven with Charles Sims, or from a more general 'broken health' in Darling's case, the war was understood to play a large part in the early ending of their lives. These men were not suffering from 'shell shock' or what people now call 'war trauma'; they were, nonetheless, casualties of the war. Whatever the uncertainty about the immediate cause of Guy Nightingale's death, the factor of alcohol was present in both family lore and in the official record. Alcohol, and cigarettes, were part of the daily management of the war. A slug of rum was issued to the men each day, and often after (and sometimes before) engagements. In R. C. Sherriff's popular play *Journey's End*, Stanhope depends heavily on whisky.[3] There are written references to alcohol among the ephemeral papers of two of the men in *Casualty Figures*. Douglas Darling sent a runner with a field message asking for cigarettes and whisky to be sent up to him in the front line; William Tyrrell kept a note to 'dear doc' asking him to find some spirits for men who had to disinter a decomposing corpse.

The point at which drinking, or specifically drinking too much in a stressful situation, shades into a wilful form of self-destruction is frequently unclear. The contribution of alcohol to the death in 1931 of the painter William Orpen has been widely acknowledged. Orpen's fellow artist and friend, Sean Keating, was in no doubt that his premature death was the result of his war experiences. William Orpen was a gifted Irish draughtsman and painter, and quickly achieved success and celebrity in London. He volunteered as an officer in the Army Service Corps and then travelled extensively in France as a war artist. Although Orpen was best known for a huge collection of formal military portraits, he also painted many moving pictures of injured, shell-shocked and dead soldiers, many of which were censored for the duration of the war itself [see Fig. 2]. He was shocked by what he saw on the western front, and he was appalled at the many unburied or only partially buried corpses. Orpen became disillusioned with politicians, and very conscious of the suffering of the fighting men. In 1916 Keating tried to persuade Orpen not to join the British army but to go back to Ireland with him, to paint. Orpen said no: he would not actually fight but he would do what he could. Keating commented bitterly, after Orpen's death at the age of 53, on what had taken the place of a creative life painting on the Aran Islands – 'the horrors of trench war, blockhead generals, political crooks and rich Americans, and finally two bottles of whiskey a day, amnesia and death at 52'.[4] Keating's interpretation is a little crude, as Orpen's drinking may also have been covering a problem with syphilis, but there can be no doubt that the conditions on the western front, even for a man not in danger, played a part in the breakdown of his health. William Orpen, visual chronicler of the war, also became another of its casualties.

It is difficult to determine accurately how many ex-soldiers died young. Anecdotal evidence suggests that quite a few did, with suicide and alcoholism mentioned most often. Fenton's study of 3,000 shell-shocked American soldiers, assessed from the end of the war until 1925, discovered that six years after the war approximately 10 per cent of them were unemployable and another 10 per cent moderately incapacitated. Looking at this small American sample, only 80 per cent had more or less recovered by 1925. Taking another indicator, nearly 115,000 'shell-shocked' ex-servicemen went through the British Army Pensions system, between 1919 and 1929, classified under 'war-related neurasthenia'. In 1939, the Ministry of Pensions was still parting with over £2 million per year under the heading of 'chronic' neurasthenia.

Most striking of all, though, was the phenomenon of 'shell shock'. The public image of shell shock has for some while been influenced by the archive film *War Neuroses* shot at Netley Hospital (and partially at Seale Hayne Hospital) in 1917. Whenever a TV documentary on the subject of shell shock appears, so too will some clips from this film. Netley Hospital had considerable success in treating men with 'hysterical' symptoms – typically such men could not walk or talk, although there was nothing physically preventing them from doing so. This was understood, loosely following Freud's ideas, as the 'conversion' of an unbearable mental wound into a physical symptom. At Netley Hospital these men were hypnotized and treated with 'suggestion', as well as offered physical massage and so on. According to the archive footage, the success rate was dramatic: they would film a man admitted to the hospital struggling to walk, who had been like that for some while; the next inter-title would say 'after 25 minutes of treatment' and then would follow footage of him walking much better. These images are widely reproduced, even though the diagnostic categories used were eccentric, to say the least. The Netley staff would observe the pathology of a man's walking difficulty and hit upon a label for it. If he looked as if he were battling against a strong wind, they would call it 'battling with the wind' gait; if he looked as though he were struggling with walking on ice, they would call it 'slippery ice' gait; and so on.

Pat Barker's *Regeneration* novels have made us more familiar with another method of curing these hysterical illnesses, one more controversial than hypnosis. In the first novel, *Regeneration* and yet more graphically in the 1997 film, we see the contrast between a kindly Dr W. H. R. Rivers, who talks sympathetically to his shell-shocked and war-weary patients, and a more brutal colleague (modelled on Dr Lewis Yealland) who is depicted using electric shocks to force a mute man to speak. The talking cure is contrasted with a form of treatment looking too close to torture to be comfortable. Both these doctors, however, have the same aim – to get their patients well enough to go back to the front.[5]

'Shell shock' was a vexed category. It was originally diagnosed by C. S. Myers, an army doctor on the western front, and coined in a paper in *The Lancet* in 1915.[6] The idea was that a soldier caught in the proximity of a bursting shell could suffer hidden injuries that were the cause of subsequent dysfunctions of mind and body. As the war progressed, psychological problems became more widespread and various ideas about shell shock were often used to explain them. The notion of an organic cause persisted; for example, both of the army doctors in *Casualty Figures* refer to concussion and other physical factors that might account for mental collapse. William Tyrrell and Lawrence Gameson each recorded instances of men who had died with not a mark on them to show why. This was proof, they thought, of the existence of a condition called at the time 'fatal shell shock'. The idea of a physical cause for shell shock was never really banished, and it found its way into the invidious distinction between what was called 'Shell Shock (W)' and 'Shell Shock (S)'. The (W) stood for wounded and was a good diagnosis to have – the soldier got to wear a wound stripe on his uniform and eventually was in an advantageous position for a pension. The (S) – for sick – was not: it laid the soldier open to hints of malingering, and stood in the way of later compensation. Army doctors were circulated with instructions about how important it was to reduce the number of cases diagnosed as

'Shell Shock (W)'; both Tyrrell and Gameson comment on these in their papers.

After the war the authorities tried to investigate shell shock, with an official committee of inquiry. Chaired by Lord Southborough, it published its findings in 1922. The committee took evidence from all the main players, including many of those responsible for treating the psychological disorders that the war had thrown up. William Tyrrell, by then representing the Medical Service of the Royal Air Force, declared in his lengthy submission that the term itself was misleading. 'Shell shock', he said, was 'an unfortunate and costly error in nomenclature'. It was costly because it offered a new escape route to the faint-hearted; Tyrrell preferred the old regime. Before the days of 'shell shock', he argued, 'the unspoken but very evident scorn of the old soldiers acted as a wholesome deterrent to all but the genuine cases of nervous breakdown'.[7] The committee agreed with him. Their first and most general recommendation was that 'The term shell-shock should be eliminated from official nomenclature, the disorders hitherto included under this heading being designated by the recognised medical terms for such conditions.'[8] Official nomenclature and popular use of language are very different, and 'shell shock' has passed into common English usage in Britain. 'Shell shock' captured, as no other expression has done so successfully, the psychological damage of war itself.

The most famous literary example of shell shock is the character of Septimus Warren Smith in Virginia Woolf's *Mrs Dalloway*, first published in 1925. Septimus has been dislocated by his experiences as a soldier in the First World War, in particular, we are told, by the experience of having his friend Evans shot down by his side.[9] He has learned not to feel, to dissociate from the event, as many soldiers did. As Wilfred Owen put it in his poem 'Insensibility',

Happy are men who yet before they are killed
Can let their veins run cold.[10]

Septimus could not get the feeling back when the war was over; he has become permanently dissociated in civilian and personal life. After being persecuted by ghastly doctors and psychiatrists, Septimus jumps from an upstairs window and dies, impaled on the railings beneath. Woolf's novel drew on personal experience. In early December 1917 Leonard Woolf's brothers Cecil and Philip, who were very close, were in action together when they were hit by a shell. Cecil was killed and Philip wounded. Visiting Philip in hospital on 14 December, Virginia Woolf speculated in her diary that 'I suppose to Philip these days pass in a dream from which he finds himself detached. I can imagine that he is puzzled why he doesn't feel more.' Emotional detachment in the face of death was familiar to Woolf, and she ascribed it to many characters in her novels. In *The Years*, Delia thinks at her mother's funeral 'None of us feel anything at all . . . we're all pretend-ing.'[11] The figure of Septimus Warren Smith was not, in any case, an attempt to describe only the shell shock of the war, as Woolf made him stand for insanity more generally. Many of the symptoms attributed to Septimus in the novel, such as hearing sparrows talking in Greek, were taken from Woolf's own break-downs. Septimus is in one sense an exploration of shell shock, but his insanity carries a more general weight. For Woolf herself, according to her diary, the novel counterposed the fictional 'truth' of Clarissa Dalloway with the 'insane truth' represented by Septimus.

The elusive nature of the term 'shell shock', which slides from the specific experiences of men in the trenches of the First World War to an expression of a more vague malaise, is illustrated by many of the men whose stories are told in *Casualty Figures*. William Tyrrell shows us both the literal and the more complex workings of what is called shell shock. Tyrrell had a breakdown in late 1915. His regiment – he was then the medical officer of the 2nd Battalion of the Lancashire Fusiliers – had been deci-mated in three encounters. Tyrrell was sent on leave before the next big push; he 'lived life to the full' in Belfast and in London, thinking it would be his last chance. On his return, they went into action, he experienced the worst shelling of the war, his regiment was again slaughtered, he was buried alive and reported dead. He broke down in tears, which he could not control. He was sent back, to work in a hospital far away from the front line, and given a period of rest for six months. Tyrrell made a complete recovery, and indeed became something of an expert on the topic of shell shock (hence was later called as a medical witness to give evidence to the committee of inquiry). Tyrrell's papers, available in the Imperial War Museum's collection of personal documents, show a lifelong professional concern with fear and courage. These files bulge with his copies of books, papers, reviews on the subject, decisively annotated and sidelined in his characteristic heavy blue crayon.

Tucked away in the family's papers is another story, that of his brother Marcus. Two of William Tyrrell's brothers, both in the Royal Flying Corps, were killed in June 1918. Alexander's death was brave and honourable: the local papers ran stories headed 'Wonderful Endurance' and 'How Capt. Tyrrell Died'.[12] He got his plane home despite having been shot in the chest, crashing within a few miles of his base. But the death of Marcus, who when younger had been the golden boy of the family, was very different. After Marcus's death, William received a letter from his father, saying that 'the circumstances of Marcus's death are tragic in the extreme . . . He was not in a fit condition for flying . . . .' As early as 1915 it had been clear that Marcus could not manage. His letters to his parents frankly set out his fears. He was in the Irish Fusiliers and could not handle being under fire; he could not return to the line. Seconded to the Flying Corps, he longed for a flesh wound that would get him out of it. He told his father than on one flight he stuck his foot over a hole in the plane in the hope that a bullet would get it. By late 1916 William was engineering a medical board to get Marcus some extended leave. Marcus's story is also a story of shell shock, but a much sadder one than

William Tyrrell's. Shortly after Alexander's death, his own
plane fell to the ground from a mere 100 yards up: the
'accident' was never explained.

Air Vice-Marshal Sir William Tyrrell was ostensibly a very
successful survivor of the war. Mastering his own encounter with
shell shock was part of a career in which he got the better of his
war experience in general. All this was done at a price. When his
marriage disintegrated twenty-five years later, his angry wife put
in writing her analysis of the causes of what she regarded as his
impossible behaviour. In a prominent position on that list was
'Nervous strain of the first war'. Declaring that she would not
live with 'a public hero', she told him that his cruelty to their
children came from the fact that 'you must kill everything in
order to be alive yourself'.

William Tyrrell is the highest ranking and most decorated
officer in this book. Ronald Skirth started the war as a corporal,
the middle of the Artillery's three non-commissioned officer
grades of bombardier, corporal and sergeant. He ended it
demoted to bombardier. Between Tyrrell and Skirth in military
rank were three junior officers. After his time in Gallipoli with
the Engineers, Willis Brown was commissioned as a lieutenant in
the Royal Field Artillery; Douglas Darling got his much-antici-
pated captaincy at the very end of the war; and Dr Lawrence
Gameson was promoted from lieutenant to captain early on. It is
a cliché of thinking about shell shock to see hysterical illnesses
such as paralysis or mutism as the fate of the ranking men, the
privates and Tommies, whereas the officers are presented as
suffering from general nervous debility, sometimes referred to as
'neurasthenia'. This small group of men, whose lives can be
looked at in some detail here, do not bear this out. Several of
these officers did not suffer mainly or only from psychological
symptoms during or after the war — it made them physically ill.
Willis Brown's history of ill health would fill a medical textbook.
Ronald Skirth suffered from the skin disease psoriasis. Douglas
Darling never recovered his health after the war. Lawrence

Gameson, too, had bouts of hospitalization towards the end of the war.

Ronald Skirth's story illustrates some of the dangers in making too sharp a division between officers and the men in the ranks. He occupied, for much of the war, a role which gave him considerable independence. He was the observer for a siege battery, stationed in the mountainous terrain of northern Italy. He had map-reading skills and had learned some Italian and was given the job of mapping the front ahead of them. He would often go off into the mountains for twenty-four hours at a time on his own. He was free of the responsibilities of a more senior officer, but he had a freedom of movement that the gunners in the ranks did not. Having made considerable use of his ambiguous position during the war, Ronald Skirth exploited it shamelessly on his train journey back from Italy to the UK when he was demobilized. He unpicked the NCO's chevron from his greatcoat but left it on his uniform. If he wanted to be a ranker, he put the coat on; if an officer, he left it off. Dr Lawrence Gameson too was able to escape the constraints of military discipline, to some extent. As a medical officer he had what he called 'a roving commission' – he was free to travel on his own to do the rounds of the two batteries for which he was responsible. Gameson felt that this solitude saved his life on several occasions, for one simple reason: men in groups had to look brave and unconcerned; a man on his own could devote his attention to looking and listening for danger, and could take cover much more effectively. It seems likely that these freedoms, these pockets of mobility, were important in the psychological survival of these two particular men. Some of the worst mental casualties of the war were found among those who were not free to move at all. When the stalemate of the trenches ended in the spring offensives of 1918, the rates for shell shock fell sharply. It was also found that the highest rates of all for mental casualties in the war, came from those who were tethered in observation balloons above the front lines. These men, sometimes called 'balloonatics', have been likened to goats staked out as tiger-bait, and proved to be the only branch of the services in which psychiatric casualties outnumbered the physically wounded.

The mental stress of war is often thought about in terms of a conflict between fear and duty: the soldier has to fight an internal battle in which his instinct for self-preservation has to be subordinated and controlled by military discipline. This struggle is clearly apparent in the life stories related here. But there was another battle going on, one which war historians such as Eric Leed have commented on, but which rises insistently and repeatedly from these men's detailed ac-counts at the time, and haunts their later memories. It was not fear; it was horror. It was not fear of the battle in prospect, or fear of their own death (though that was obviously present), but horror, often nauseated, at the battle just gone. In parti-cular, it was about the bodies, damaged but alive, and the dead ones. Willis Brown's last memory, before his amnesiac break-down, was of being in a trench full of dead Turks. Ronald Skirth gave graphic descriptions of the distended dead bodies he encountered at Messines and at Ypres and the part they played in his shell shock. Douglas Darling spared his fiancée these details in his letters, but he wrote of the depression he could not shake off when much later he found human remains, and the 'desolation and loneliness' of death, on the battlefield at Vimy Ridge. Lawrence Gameson, not writing for publication, of course, gave detailed descriptions of the decomposition of human bodies.

William Tyrrell's papers reveal an example of how little these experiences were understood at home. For his submission to the 1922 Committee Inquiry on Shell Shock he was sent lists of possible causes of the condition, mainly related to fear and stress, and asked to comment on them. Tyrrell agreed with this emphasis in a general way, as he believed that the primary cause of shell shock was the repression of fear – the constant effort men were making not to show their fear. He thought that the fear of being found afraid was a 'grandparent' of shell shock. But he added 'mud and blood' and 'nauseating sights and smells' to the list of causes. His evidence, which was reproduced at some length in the final report, included the following passage: 'Next comes severe mental stress grouped with fatigue, mud and blood, wet and cold, misery and monotony, unsavoury cooking and feeding, nauseating environment, etc.' Sights and smells have been converted to 'environment', which is different and much weaker.

The men exposed to nauseating sights and smells were quite insistent about this: it was not an 'environment' that they were in – they absorbed it through their own bodily senses. Descriptions of Gallipoli invariably emphasize the problem of the corpses. They were not stacked up somewhere else, just to be looked at; they were physically encountered in the most direct way. Guy Nightingale described one such moment, on 10 May 1915, in a letter to his mother. Ordered to make a forward movement at night, they advanced to a place where there had been a battle two weeks earlier in which around 2,000 men had died.

> These bodies were still lying there highly decomposed and the stench was awful. In the dark we kept tumbling over the bodies and treading on them. When it was light I found that I had dug in next to the remains of an officer in the KOSB [King's Own Scottish Borderers] whom I had last seen at the Opera in Malta and had spent a most jolly evening with.

A. P. Herbert's novel *The Secret Battle*, which draws on his own experiences in Gallipoli in 1915, also dwells on the physical immediacy of the corpses in their trenches: 'But there was a hideous fascination about the things, so that after a few hours a man came to know the bodies in his bay with a sickening intimacy, and could have told you many details about each of them . . .'[13] Later, in his autobiography, Herbert said that he reread the Gallipoli section of the book, after fifty years: 'It gives,

I felt, a veracious picture of daily life on the front-line on the Gallipoli Peninsula. I saw, I heard, I smelt it all again.'[14]

William Orpen, in a book about his work as a war artist, *An Onlooker in France*, remembered an officer asking him if he could paint the Somme. 'Paint the Somme?' he responded. 'I could do it from memory – just a flat horizon-line and mud-holes and water, with the stumps of a few battered trees,' he said, 'but one could not paint the smell.'[15] The smell of the Somme, as that of Gallipoli, was the smell of decomposition, of corpses that had not been dealt with. This included the carcasses of horses and mules, but the human remains were the most disturbing to Orpen. In a letter to his friend Henry Tonks, he described a battlefield three weeks on: 'they have now started to bury the dead in some parts of it, German and English mixed, this consists of throwing some mud over the bodies as they lie, they don't even worry to cover them altogether, arms and feet showing in lots of cases.'[16]

An unfinished Orpen painting makes clear that he saw a connection between the unburied corpses and insanity. This is *The Mad Woman of Douai*, which he began to paint in 1918 [see Fig. 3]. The picture remains eerily green in its underpainted, rough state; a corpse in the left foreground has received a mockery of a burial, one foot not even covered by the earth dumped on top of it. The mad woman of the title stares beyond the inadequately buried corpse, her eyes neither focused nor coordinated, her splayed knees an allusion to the sexual violence of war. The image captures something of the shocking reality of decomposing corpses, and their psychological effects on the people, usually men, who had to live with them. The painting points to a link between mental breakdown and the profound unease we feel when corpses are not treated properly.

One war artist more than any other found a way to paint the human destruction of the western front: Paul Nash, most popular of the British war artists, and a painter whose vision of the front has coloured British imagination and memory of the war. Paul Nash painted the butchered trees, not the people. The dismembered trees function as a metaphor for the damaged human bodies, but we do not have to look at them directly; they are implied in the landscape. Nash's work enables the viewer to draw a parallel between the trees and the bodies. We can imagine, but do not have to see, the destroyed bodies we know to be there under the dead trees.

Nash left the Slade Art School in 1911, dissatisfied with his progress. He was no good at figure drawing; he was not able to represent the human form. He did not think it worth wasting more money on an art education. Later, he realized that he had a different talent. Walking in the country one day, he recounted the exact moment:

> I would draw this tree in front of me as I felt it. It was exciting drawing this tree thrusting up out of the hedge . . . The spring sunlight struck across the wide shoulders of the oak, glancing down its great limbs which reflected the beams in a pale glow: the round trunk in the sunlight was as white as paper. I did not find it difficult to draw this tree, as I had found the models at the Slade difficult to draw. An instinctive knowledge seemed to serve me as I drew, enabling my hand to convey my understanding. I could make these branches grow as I could never make the legs and arms of the models move and live.
>
> There stole through me a peculiar thrill as I realized the forms taking life under my hand.[17]

Nash was anthropomorphic about trees – this oak tree had 'wide shoulders' and 'great limbs'. He endowed them with human attributes. In a letter to his wife Margaret, from the front, he described the scene: 'In the distance runs a stream where the stringy poplars and alders lean about dejectedly, while farther a slope rises to a scarred bluff the foot of which is scattered with headless trees standing white and withered, hopeless, without any leaves, done, dead.'[18] Nash's extraordinary talent in painting trees made him a wonderful landscape painter. His pre-war pictures of the English countryside are worthy successors to the vision of Samuel Palmer. When he went to the front, he was struck by 'the strange beauty of war', a beauty that had no reference to human suffering:

> The willows are orange, the poplars carmine with buds, the streams gleam brightest blue and flights of pigeons go wheeling about the field. Mixed up with all this normal beauty of nature you see the strange beauty of war. Trudging along the road you become gradually aware of a humming in the air, a sound rising and falling in the wind. You look up and after a second's search you can see a gleaming shaft in the blue like a burnished silver dart, another and then another. Then comes a new noise, two or three cracks from somewhere in the near farms, a second, and as you gaze the blue sky is charmingly speckled by little shining clouds of white. Nothing could be gayer, the clear blue pierced by silver darts and spangled with baby clouds. Nothing whiter, purer, more full of life than these flaky clouds.[19]

This was not to last. Famously, Paul Nash became violently disillusioned. He was, he said to Margaret, 'no longer an artist', but had become 'a messenger' from the fighting men to those who were prolonging the war – his message was, he said, 'a bitter truth' that should 'burn their lousy souls'.[20] He turned his imagination to the effect of the war on his beloved trees. Nash's paintings of the desolation of the western front are not landscapes of war with no reference to human suffering. They work by putting the humans into the background rather than by excluding them. In *Void,* for example, the humans are present in the tiny aeroplanes in the sky, and in the flattened corpse in the foreground [see Fig. 4]. Paul Nash found a visual language to depict the horrors of the front, but one that allows the viewer not to confront them directly. It is this that made his work so successful, and so influential.

During the war itself, artists were not allowed to show the casualties of war. Depiction of dead human bodies was banned in 1917. Earlier on, things had been more flexible, but when packed cinemas across the country showed footage of British soldiers burying German bodies on the battlefield, in the official 1916 film of *The Battle of the Somme*, it was found shocking. Day after day the letters page of *The Times* returned to the vexed issue of whether the film was fit for public exhibition. The king had majority opinion on his side when he declared that the public 'should see these pictures' so that they learned 'what war means'.[21] But the Dean of Durham objected, saying the film 'violates the very sanctities of bereavement'.[22] Another correspondent likened the film to watching 'the hangings at Newgate and the flogging of the madmen at Bedlam'; 'mere curiosity' serving as 'a pretext for witnessing scenes of agony'.[23] The film was one of only two, both made in 1916, that showed dead bodies; by the following year public opinion was swinging against the war and corpses were deemed bad for military morale.

These controversial scenes, which show the decent burial of intact and fresh corpses whose faces the camera avoids, are a long way from the more disturbing old or mutilated remains the soldiers had to deal with. It has been calculated that in the First World War an average of 5,600 soldiers died every day. The corpses were more of a problem in some places than in others. The terrain at Gallipoli made burials difficult; the defence of Verdun is another extreme case. Successive waves of men died on top of each other, defending narrow paths in the hills, and this resulted in very large quantities of unidentifiable French (and German) bones. Eventually the bones of an estimated 130,000 men were collected up and buried, simply according to the sector of the battlefield where they had been found, in the huge 'ossuary' at Douaumont.

If the corpses of the battlefields were difficult for the men who had to deal with them, what could the home front cope with seeing? The work of the war artists was censored – the job of

Major Arthur Lee, who quickly became a personal enemy of the painter C. R. W. Nevinson. At the end of 1917 Lee refused permission for Nevinson's painting *The Paths of Glory*, depicting two dead British soldiers, to be shown in public in wartime. The censor's ruling was clear, since 'the War Office, on military grounds, has prohibited the appearance of dead bodies, even Germans, in any official photograph or film'. The official correspondence with Nevinson adds that 'Photographs of this kind are now rigidly suppressed.'[24] Nevinson, confident that higher authorities would overrule the censor (as they had just done for another of his paintings), had the painting hung in the Leicester Galleries in London for the opening of his 'Pictures of War' exhibition in March 1918. When they didn't relent, Nevinson simply covered the two bodies with a strip of brown paper saying 'Censored', and left the painting in the show, attracting much press attention and an official reprimand. To the commisioners of British war art, a German corpse was, in practice, more acceptable than a British one. Only two months later, in May, William Orpen was given permission to exhibit a painting of two corpses, one with a decomposing face, entitled *Dead Germans in a Trench*.

Unlike Paul Nash, Orpen was extremely good at drawing people, so good that he was able to command a very large income from it. In the late 1920s he earned more than £45,000 a year, charging £2,000 for a full-length picture. During the war, Orpen painted many portraits of military people, a huge collection of top brass and generals; but also others – commissioned for propaganda purposes – of young men in the Flying Corps and so on. His ability to capture a likeness was striking. Lieutenant Rhys Davids, a very dashing young pilot who had been school captain at Eton, was killed very shortly after being painted by Orpen. His mother wrote to say that 'it is . . . extraordinarily like him in his thoughtful moods and such as no hasty photographer ever got near reproducing', adding that the painting was 'a lasting treasure and the solitary ray of comfort'.[25] Less well known than his official portraits are the paintings – many of them censored during the war – that Orpen made of what he saw at the front when he went in 1917–18 to France as a war artist. Corpses – mostly human, but sometimes of animals – were shown in many of these paintings. Orpen's censored images of corpses on the western front are the other side of the coin of Paul Nash's destroyed landscapes. For the men on the ground, the human bodies were inescapable.

Early in the morning of 7 June 1917, approximately 10,000 German troops were blown up when the nineteen mines laid under their front line at Messines Ridge were simultaneously detonated. The blast could be heard in London. The next day, Ronald Skirth was with a party of three others from his artillery unit going forward to the old German trenches. Amid the human wreckage he found a perfect body. 'What I saw might have been a life-size wax model of a German soldier.' The body was leaning back, resting against the edge of a small shell hole; he looked as if he had simply fallen asleep. 'There was no blood-stain, no bruise visible either on his person or uniform.' His posture, to Skirth, looked perfectly natural and normal. His helmet was slightly tilted back, and a lock of blond hair rested on his forehead. Ronald Skirth was 19, but this boy looked young-er. In his hand was a wallet, open at two small photographs, one presumably of his parents, the other a teenage girl who could have been the 'twin sister' of Ron's girlfriend Ella. That picture was inscribed 'Mein Hans'. The young Ronald felt instantly that he identified with the German boy. He concluded that 'he must have died of shell shock' rather than from the mine explosions, as his body was undamaged. He soon made the connection that he himself had been firing shells in the attack the day before. Could one of his own shells have killed Hans? For Ronald Skirth, finding Hans's body was a turning point in his attitude to the war. 'My adolescence ended that day', he declared, for he knew that he would have to live his life with a troubled conscience.

Ronald Skirth had encountered what was thought at the time to be a phenomenon of 'fatal shell shock'. William Tyrrell, as it happens, was also on the battlefield at Messines Ridge shortly after the mines blew up. His description, later given to the shell shock inquiry, was very different in style from Skirth's, but he found something similar. He visited the site within two hours of the mine explosions, in which, as he put it, 'debris and bodies were evulsed from a depth of sixty feet', a depth later proved correct by analysis of the soil strata thrown up. Tyrrell found 'dead Germans, three in number, lying unsoiled – unmarked – one with spectacles still on and unbroken – no visible sign or evidence of violence'. Tyrrell excluded the possibility of gas, as 'the eyes and pupils were normal', although the committee correctly noted that carbon monoxide poisoning was a possibility. Using the then-common distinction between 'emotional' and 'commotional' shock, Tyrrell concluded that he had found a classic instance of death by 'commotional disturbance without visible injury'. He had seen other cases of this, but 'none so definite or so well proved'.[26]

Many attempts were made to try and determine the cause of these unexplained deaths. Analysis of the brains of men killed by shell concussion in France had revealed 'punctiform' haemorrhages in the white matter, also typical of death by carbon monoxide poisoning. Had these men been exposed to this gas as well as being shelled? Other doctors had by means of post-mortem lumbar punctures found changes in the cerebrospinal fluid, indicating damage to the central nervous system. In 1917, Lawrence Gameson, who had an interest in medical pathology, found a case of fatal shell shock in his own artillery battery, the 71st Royal Field Artillery. The forward section, of two guns, was located behind Prue Copse, at Middle Wood on the Somme. Dr Gameson described the scene:

The mess was of stock design: square hole dug in the ground, roofed with some head-cover, walls lined with heavy planks and connected to the battery by a short trench. The enemy

got a direct hit on the entrance with a 5.9. The two officers
were alone in the mess when the shell burst. All the heavy
planks were displaced sideways by the explosion. Farrington
escaped with a very severe shaking, but his companion was
killed instantly. I examined him almost immediately after
death. I could find no external signs whatever of the cause
of death. He did not die of carbon monoxide poisoning,
because Farrington would almost certainly have been affected
as well. He was killed by shock, by concussion.

Gameson recorded that he was 'sorely tempted' to do a post-
mortem, as he did not know what tissues had been damaged. But
he was not in a hospital and military protocol in the field
suggested otherwise: 'if a man was dead as a result of enemy
action he was dead, and that was that'.

'Fatal shell shock' produced a troubling body, one that was
outwardly perfect. The man was dead, but those who saw him
could not tell how, or why, he had died. Enigmatic and slightly
uncanny, the phenomenon affected those who encountered it.
The two army doctors in this book recorded it as a conundrum of
medical pathology. For Ronald Skirth, in June 1917, it was the first
corpse that he felt was a person, like himself but dead, rather than a
thing. Skirth's previous experiences of corpses had been distressing
in a different way – they were the 'things' that were left when men,
and animals such as horses and mules, had been blown to pieces,
dismembered, distended. In those cases it was all too clear what the
cause of death had been. Later that year, Skirth was to encounter
many more corpses, in his retreat during the battle of Third Ypres.
There were 'unending shell-holes nearly all containing horrific
things that had once been parts of men and animals'. Thinking
back to the 'ghastly horror of the sights and smells we had to live
with' in that period, he said later that 'I am still amazed that I was
able to endure them so long without losing my reason'.

These experiences were the beginning of Skirth's amnesia, and
his breakdown two months later. Another soldier to record a

connection between the ubiquitous corpses and mental breakdown was Ebenezer Fairbrother, a private in the Coldstream
Guards. Fairbrother was also at Ypres, for the first of the battles
there. On 31 October 1914 he noted in his diary:

> We dig trenches close to a race course but have to go and
> relieve the 7th Division at Zillibeke and we dig in outside a
> village. A lot of German dead lay around here. A burning
> farm-house lit up the country for miles around. One of our
> fellows went mad and was taken away.

On 7 November 'the woods in front were thick with unburied
Germans', and at the end of that month 'there are hundreds of
dead Germans lying in front'. In February 1915, near Bethune,
'we were told to dig graves in the darkness, but we started
getting up arms and legs and then a head, so I gave it up for I
could not do it; the smell was abominable'. Later that year, at
the Battle of Loos, Fairbrother recorded 'there are dead bodies
lying everywhere; both ours and Germans. What an awful
sight.' Shortly after that he was 'asked to take the stripes today
but refuse as I think I would rather remain a Tommy.' Fairbrother was eventually invalided out with shell shock, and sent
to the Maudsley Hospital. In April 1918 he commented in his
laconic style, 'No one here seems to own me, but it seems,
according to my documents, I have been sent home 'war worn'
Army orders.'

Douglas Darling did not tell his beloved fiancée in Folkestone any of these kinds of things. We know now that the
barrage in which he participated, on the day that the Canadians took Vimy Ridge, was not merely an important military
victory but a gruesome experience by any standards. Eleven
thousand men whose bodies were never identified are commemorated on the memorial at Vimy. There had been so
much fighting beforehand that the advance went forward over
the corpses of many men. Knowing what was coming, Dou-

glas wrote to Bee, 'Don't forget to pray for me, dear heart, trying times are coming and I will need all my courage to face the music.' Before and after the attack he told her that his 'nerves are bad', but of the day itself he wrote 'it has been a glorious day for the Canadians'. Shortly afterwards, he wrote, 'my hair is falling out very badly'. Darling was taking the strain without being able to explain it fully to her. In this he was not unusual.

Lawrence Gameson was exercised about how much of the 'beastliness' of the war he should preserve; he specifically used that word to refer to corpses. His photo albums, which do contain some images of corpses, were a focus of this anxiety. Over the years he changed the captions of some pictures, as his views on this question changed. But as he thought his memoir would never be published, he did not have the same anxiety about the written descriptions of his work as a doctor. Yet the passages where he wrote about necrosis, and particularly the descriptions of maggot invasion in the tissue of living men, are perhaps the most shocking of all.

Willis Brown was invalided out of the Gallipoli campaign, ill with dysentery and suffering from shell shock. At Gallipoli the problem of unburied corpses was so severe that at the end of May 1915 a short ceasefire was negotiated for burial of the dead. A twenty-four-hour truce, carefully policed, enabled some mass graves to be dug and filled. The corpses at Gallipoli were directly linked, in the family account of Willis Brown's case, to his mental frailty. Pushing the link further, those corpses have been invoked – in fiction – as an explanation of the mental state that led to an execution for cowardice. A. P. Herbert's novel *The Secret Battle* contains dramatic descriptions of decomposing corpses. The ninth edition, in 1949, carries an introductory note by Winston Churchill, to the effect that the tale is 'founded on fact'. Herbert fictionalized, in the character of Harry Penrose, the fate of the real-life Edwin Dyett, who was executed on the western front for desertion. A volunteer officer of the Royal Naval Division,

Dyett had lost his nerve and was found running away from the front, court-martialled and shot. He has been seen as a man who was executed for war trauma, a psychological casualty who was treated with punitive military discipline.

Dyett's case was publicised in the *John Bull* newspaper in 1918; he was one of only three officers executed during the war. A. P. Herbert had a close connection to the case: an officer in the same Royal Naval Division (the 63rd), he was (according to his biographer) shaken 'to the heart's core' by what happened to Dyett.[27] Herbert had actually taken part in the action in which Dyett's courage failed: 435 men attacked the village of Beaucourt, but only about twenty of them survived. A. P. Herbert went through the disastrous Gallipoli campaign of 1915, before being invalided out, whereas Dyett only joined the battalion after they were evacuated in early 1916. According to Leonard Sellers, Herbert had not only been there in the battle at Beaucourt: he was also probably asked if he would act as the 'prisoner's friend' in the court martial that followed (as he had legal training), but he declined.[28] Herbert's strategy in *The Secret Battle* was to use his own memories of Gallipoli to explain Penrose's mental breakdown on the Western Front. Rotting corpses are the worst problem. Things begin to go wrong when Harry decides to sleep on the floor of a trench where, our narrator sees ('in a moment of nauseating insight'), there are maggots from the French and Turkish bodies not far beneath him. 'Rubbish', says Harry, 'they're glow worms resting.'

Harry's mental decline is associated in the novel with guilt about the deaths of men under his command, and a less tangible, somewhat uncanny, experience of corpses. One incident combines the two themes. A shell hits a section of the trench parapet and Harry moves the four men of that bay into the next one, unfortunately putting eight men straight into the path of a shell. Six of Harry's men are killed. A mere two hours later, they have unfathomably decomposed into black, reeking, fly-ridden corpses – as if they have been dead for weeks. They look like the bodies of enemy Turks, and Harry cannot identify any of his men by name. 'I hope', says the narrator, 'I may never again see such horror as was in Harry's face.'

Harry ends up being invalided out of Gallipoli with dysentery, but before that happens, the narrator of the story (a soldier colleague of Harry's) takes the opportunity to expand on the problem of dead bodies. He describes their unit being moved forward to an area that has recently seen a huge battle; there are corpses everywhere, hanging over and into the trenches they now occupy. As they can only bury them at night, they have to live with them. He tells us that men are constantly being sent away, stricken with nausea, by the doctor; that it is the only thing worse than the front line. Even the prospect of battle becomes more attractive than staying there – 'anything was welcome if we could get out of that trench, away from the smell and the flies, away from those bodies . . .'[29]

A. P. Herbert was a very successful man: trained in the law, he became a prolific and popular writer, an MP for Oxford University, and was knighted in 1945. *The Secret Battle*, published in 1919, is markedly different from his direct and cheerful prose and verse. The book was written amid horrible nightmares, according to Herbert himself, but it served its function of exorcizing the experience, and his inevitable guilt. He had, some would say, laid the ghost to rest by writing the novel. He was particularly proud that the book, read by David Lloyd George and Winston Churchill, subsequently played a part in reform of the system of courts martial.

Another man who used his professional skills as a writer to work through his personal experience of the war was Rudyard Kipling. The story of John Kipling's death in 1915 is well known, as is his father's involvement in the Imperial (now Commonwealth) War Graves Commission. In the years following John's death, Kipling undertook two major tasks. The first was a regimental history of the Irish Guards, his son's regiment, a two-volume work of extensive military and historical scholarship, and one for which Kipling, other than by virtue of his son's

death, would not have been an obvious choice. For the War
Graves Commission, his work was tireless. He became the arbiter
of every inscription – not just the major ones with which his
name is associated, such as 'Their Name Liveth for Evermore'
and 'A British Soldier Known Unto God', but all others, no
matter how small. A trawl through the archives of the Commission reveals a continual correspondence in which Kipling selected inscriptions particular to every individual place and
circumstance. When Kipling died in 1936, the Commission
put on record that every inscription around the world had been
'written, approved or selected' by him.[30] When Reginald
Blomfield, the architect of the Menin Gate, rashly inserted his
own possible inscription into the drawings in 1923, there was a
flurry of correspondence lest Kipling might feel he was being
sidelined. He replied, 'I always considered that all inscriptions
came my way sooner or later, and the Menin gate one is
especially to be thought over. I expect Blomfield, as you say,
put the words in for the look of his sketch.'

The story of John Kipling has left a divisive legacy. Rejected
on medical grounds – he had terrible eyesight – his father called
in a favour and got John a commission in the Irish Guards. He
was killed at the age of 18 during his first hours in action, at the
Battle of Loos. Rudyard Kipling's own reputation in relation to
the war, and his association with empire generally, has made his
son's death a battleground for intrusive platitudes, both about
his grief and his responsibility for the boy's death. More
significant is the fact that the Kipling tragedy is one where
there was a missing body. John's body was never found in the
lifetime of his parents, who tried on many visits to France to
locate it. In 1992, the War Graves Commission named the
grave of a previously 'unknown' soldier as that of John Kipling;
it now appears that this was an error. John Kipling's body
remains unidentified, one of the missing.

The ubiquitous corpses of the First World War mirror the
missing. Willis Brown was at Gallipoli: nearly 21,000 British

troops alone are recorded on the memorial to the missing at Cape Helles cemetery. Douglas Darling was at Vimy Ridge: the names of over 11,000 missing Canadians are on the memorial there. Ronald Skirth was at the Third Battle of Ypres, and William Tyrrell at the First: the names of 54,000 men who died on the Ypres Salient but to whom 'the fortune of war denied the known and honoured burial given to their comrades in death' (Kipling's words) are on the Menin Gate. Lawrence Gameson was at the Somme: the memorial to the missing of the Somme at Thiepval contains over 70,000 names. These five survivors were in the vicinity of battlefields where over 150,000 men were killed but not identified, many of them blown to pieces. The figure for the war as a whole is estimated at nearly two million.

Many families were in the same position as the Kiplings, with no identified body and no known grave or resting place. As Kipling put it himself in his short story 'The Gardener', the families of those men who were missing had no 'altar upon earth where they might lay their love'.[31] After I started working on this project I decided to look at my own family history. One great-uncle's name is to be found on the Menin Gate, and another on the memorial at the Somme. This latter, my grandfather's younger brother Eric, was killed at High Wood in September 1916, aged 26. Eric was a bit of a joker evidently: he used to annoy his very traditional family by standing his 3-year-old niece on the kitchen table and getting her to say, 'Votes for Women!' Family records of his death seemed formal – until I came across the order of service for his mother's funeral in 1930. This was to be his funeral too, as there couldn't be one in 1916 when he died. The mourners were asked to couple her death with his, 'who on September 15th, 1916, found the "Great Peace" amid the carnage of High Wood'. Like so many other families, they had no body on which to focus their grief. It has come down through the family that when the coffin of the 'unknown warrior' of the western front was brought to London for ceremonial burial in Westminster Abbey, in 1920, his mother said 'that could be Eric in there'. As we now know, many other mothers said the same thing.

The bereaved families had to learn to live, indefinitely, with the absence of a body. The soldiers had to live, finitely, with the bodies of their friends and comrades, and the corpses of the unidentified. That experience of death was not lightly overcome. *Casualty Figures* is not about those who died in the war; it is about the way their deaths affected the lives of the survivors.

Lieutenant John Willis Brown
Royal Naval Division Engineers
Royal Field Artillery

John Willis Brown went by the name of Willis, his mother's maiden name. He was born in Sheffield in 1897, the son of a steel works manager. In 1915 he was in training with the newly formed Royal Naval Division when he fell critically ill with cerebrospinal meningitis. His family were summoned to the Naval Hospital at Deal, where they were told that they should 'pray that he might die quickly' because up till then there had been no known case of recovery without severe brain damage. From their lodgings in Deal, his mother and sister watched going past the window the funerals of the men who had died of the disease. They were allowed to watch Willis through a hospital window: he was thrashing wildly and being held down by six orderlies. But Willis Brown recovered. A mere two weeks later he was weak, but mentally unimpaired and 'furious because his unit had gone to the Dardanelles without him'.

Six weeks on, Willis went to a medical board in London and he came back 'beaming all over and saying that he was going out on a draft to Gallipoli the next day'. There he was able to rejoin his unit, a field company of the Royal Naval Division Engineers (RNDE). Willis had originally enlisted in an infantry regiment as soon as the war broke out, giving a false age as he was then only 17. His father extricated him from that, but knew that they would not for long be able to prevent him going to war. The solution was to find 'a good lot of men', and they chose 'Winston's newly formed R.N.D.E.', where his father 'knew someone'. The Royal Naval Division did not exist before the outbreak of the war. It was formed because the Admiralty calculated that they had 20–30,000 men in reserves, who could be called up when war broke out – but they had no ships to put them on. The idea was therefore to set up forces of amphibians, men who had naval training but were to function as units in the army. The Royal Marine Brigade was formed in 1914, and brigades of Navy reservists were established too. The Royal Naval Division remained under Admiralty control until April 1916, when it was transferred to the War Office. Winston Churchill, as First Sea Lord, was therefore a key figure in setting up the Division, as well as the architect of the Dardanelles campaign.

Willis Brown enlisted in the Marines in London in September 1914, adding two years again to his age, as his official parchment certificate shows. So 'off he went to camp, very happy and excited', to become a Marines Engineer. Jolly accounts survive of the RNDE camp at Walmer in Kent, including bathing at St Margaret's Bay, jaunts to the pubs of Deal, and excursions with the local 'sweeties'. But Willis Brown was joining a group of men who were also 'very impatient and anxious to go overseas'. The RNDE, consisting of three field companies, a signal company and a depot company, embarked on 1 March 1915, as part of the Mediterranean Expeditionary Force. Willis Brown joined his unit in Gallipoli, and in June 1915 he described, in the one surviving letter to his mother, the work he was doing there. He was at that stage not a commissioned officer.

> Our work at present consists of supervising the construction and improvement of trenches. We each take a working party of about fifty. It is not bad work, much better than digging yourself, but it gets very boring. Occasionally we get a job of

digging wells, bridging gullies, & making roads, which is quite a change.

Willis was digging when disaster struck. The family's account is based on his recollections afterwards, and a report from the friend of his father, a Major Morgan, who had got him into the unit. 'He had had light dysentery for a long time', said his aunt later,

> and must have been light-headed for he went on digging long after the order to retreat had been given. The last thing he could remember was finding himself alone, under heavy fire, in a trench full of dead Turks. So he shovelled them all down to one end and sat down at the other.

According to Major Morgan, 'they had given up all hope of him when, several nights later, they saw a scarecrow figure walking towards them in full moonlight and just in the nick of time, before someone shot at him, realized it was Willis, delirious and, of course, starving'. He was put on a hospital ship with other cases of enteric fever and Major Morgan cancelled the telegram he had dictated, letting his parents know that 'JWB was missing, believed killed'.

Willis Brown's experiences in the spring and summer of 1915 in Gallipoli were very common. The dysentery was widespread. A doctor serving with the Royal Naval Division, of which Willis Brown's unit was a part, later wrote that

> From a medical standpoint, this month [June] was remark-able for a large and sudden increase in sickness. Gone were the healthy days of April and May, and with the increasing heat numerous epidemics arose. Chief among these were typhoid, paratyphoid, dysentery, enteritis, jaun-dice, malaria, and that obscure condition known in the Army as P.U.O. (pyrexia of unknown origin). The 'Gal-

lipoli Gallop' was a term largely used by the men and covered any complaint of which the words are suggestive or symptomatic.

This doctor commented on the implications of these epidemics:

> The amount of sickness was so great that the Division, in spite of numerous reinforcements which continually arrived, would soon have become non-existent if every sick man had been evacuated to hospital. Hence all who could carry on at all were kept with their battalions, and treated by the battalion medical officers. The men, with a very fine *esprit de corps*, appreciated the adverse conditions under which we laboured and made light of their complaints.

In the Imperial War Museum there are two documents describing daily life in Willis Brown's field company at this point. Both are anonymous, but the characters of the two authors become quickly apparent. The first one, *Diary of No. 2 Field Company*, includes an entry for 7 June:

> Flies getting a filthy nuisance now. Simply billions of 'em everywhere. Requires some practice to take a mouthful of bread and jam without half a dozen or so following it in. Meat absolutely black with 'em and you had to keep fishing them out of the stew as you went along.

Later, the author commented that

> besides ordinary casualties we soon had a steady dribble of people sent away with dysentery. In fact everybody had it more or less and you had to be jolly bad for the M.O. [medical officer] to take any notice of you. The swarms of flies and the magnificent collection of dead Turks between the lines must have had a lot to do with it. As a result everybody went off

their feed and likewise very much off their work and it was
difficult to get an ordinary job done in less than three or four
times the usual time.

Illustrating what the doctor referred to as the great *esprit de corps*
of the men, this chap goes on:

> I have a note of a Divisional Order issued in August containing
> this delightful passage – so unlike the usual sort:- 'The G.O.C
> realizes that there is a good deal of sickness in the Division (I
> believe it was about one-third strength about then) and that
> the men are not so fit for hard work as they were, but he trusts
> that a special effort will be made . . .' He nearly said 'please'!

The second document, *With the RNDE*, is more restrained, but
gives a timely illustration of the practical problems of fighting
with such illnesses rampant. An account of a battle at the end of
June tells us that

> after a while Sammy Shields was hit and he and I went behind
> a tree and took out a field dressing with the intention of
> bandaging him up. However, the poor fellow was in agony
> with dysentery and he decided to go back to the line, where I
> left him in a latrine . . .

Willis Brown's encounter with a trench full of dead Turks was
another common experience. His last memory was of shovelling
the corpses up to one end of the trench and sitting down at the
other. The problem of unburied corpses was particularly acute at
Gallipoli. In Peter Liddle's *Men of Gallipoli* there is a vivid
summary of these conditions, from Major C. S. Black of the
Highland Light Infantry:

> On Gallipoli there were no reserves. The troops that
> stormed and carried a position had to consolidate and hold

on to the captured ground for days or it might be weeks afterwards. And what ground it was to hold on to during those sweltering July days! All around in the open lay our own dead, whom no one could approach to bury by day or night, for to climb out of the trench even in the dark was to court disaster. The trenches themselves were littered with the Turkish victims of our shellfire, in places piled on top of one another to the depth of several feet. The stench was indescribable. In one communication trench that had to be used for days until another could be cut, it was necessary to crawl on hands and knees for many yards over the reeking bodies in order to keep within shelter of the parapet. The heat was stifling both day and night; water was almost unobtainable.[1]

Willis Brown was one of many men invalided out of the Dardanelles campaign. Sent to Charing Cross Hospital in London, he was eventually driven by volunteering 'kind ladies with cars' to visit his family, then living in Sidcup. His sister Margaret wrote:

I shall never forget my first sight of him – a long emaciated creature, with great hollow eyes, a greenish-yellow skin and limbs that were all sticks and knobs; but the most extraordinary thing was his hair. His head had been shaved when he was first put to bed and it had grown, its old brown colour, about half an inch; but growing through it, making a sort of halo round his head, about an inch and a half long, was new soft golden baby-hair and the total effect was quite spectral. He had an expression of dumb horror, under his usual smile-disguise and he was willing to talk about the peculiarities of the Australian mentality; of how the King had been to see them and he had been chosen as spokesman for the ward; of the wonder of English grass and trees . . . but not of anything else.

Margaret's memoir included information about Willis's parents
and grandparents. His father was a successful businessman, a
practical man who did not understand the complex and philo-
sophical temperament that several of his children had inherited
from their mother's side of the family.

> Willis would think out something really very clever that he
> was not technically equipped to make, so of course it didn't
> work in performance and Father would laugh at him and say
> 'that's a soft sort of thing to waste time and materials on'
> without bothering to find out what he had been aiming at.
> Willis's mouth would quiver at the corners but he'd laugh and
> throw the thing away.

When his mother tried to comfort him it was the last thing he
wanted: 'He'd say "Father was right. It wasn't good", and run
away.' His mother emerges as a woman who tried to compensate
for her husband's hardness by 'showing off' the children's
accomplishments wherever possible. They all hated it, especially
Willis.

How would the family cope with Willis's return from Gallipoli in this state? In the long term, his ever-practical father was
later reported as saying that 'as Willis hadn't lost a limb or even
had a wound, he ought to think himself very lucky'. More
immediately, how was a proud and indulgent mother going to
react? It seems that she was so thankful for his return, and so
proud of him, that she wanted her friends to see her wonderful
boy on his visits home from the hospital. Although she knew that
he wanted not to talk about his experiences, she could not resist
surreptitiously inviting her friends to 'just drop in, accidentally'.
Once there they would ply him with questions. Eventually he
said, 'If one more nice lady asks me what it was like in the
Dardanelles I shall really tell her and nobody will like it at all.'
The warning wasn't enough. The next lot of nice ladies who 'just
happened to drop in' and ask their inevitable questions had them

answered. 'He told them, very quietly and calmly, horrors such as none of them had ever dreamed of and, once started he couldn't stop. He gave them the lot, and then got up and walked out to the waiting car without saying goodbye to anyone.' The next day a note arrived saying that he would rather not come home any more just yet.

'He gave them the lot.' The experiences Willis told them about were later described in detail. *The Diary of No. 2 Field Company* gives an impressionistic account of the conditions that Willis had been living in. On 7 June the entry reads:

> On arrival at daylight find this trench rather uninviting. Still a lot of stiffs in it from June 4th – there's one chap that the Manchesters use as a sort of sideboard to keep their jam tins on, and another bloke sitting on the parapet with a broad and beastly grin and his face quite black. And swarms of flies. Altogether very untidy.

As for the food, it was very sketchy at the beginning and later they couldn't eat it.

> Grub gradually improved as our appetites deteriorated. We started off on a diet consisting exclusively of bully (or maconochie) biscuit, bacon, plum and apple [jam], and tea (without milk, tinned or otherwise). That lasted until we could hardly look at any of it, then we got bread, later on fresh (i.e. frozen) meat and later still such luxuries as marge, rice, porridge etc. Canteens were non-existent at first, so it was impossible to buy anything else and parcels from home didn't begin to arrive for several weeks.

Food parcels figure prominently in Willis's letter to his mother in June. He asked anxiously for more parcels to be sent to him. He added, 'by the way you might encourage other people to send me letters and parcels as they are the only things to look forward to here'. 'Anyone will do', he wrote rather desperately, 'as there is quite a lot of competition as to who gets most mails, some get ten or twelve things a week regularly.' His top priority was chocolate, followed by cigarettes (tins of fifty 'Three Castles') or tobacco, Oxo cubes, toffee, books and periodicals.

The anonymous memoirist of No. 2 Company tells the story of bathing in Morto Bay, just inside the straits. 'It was a good place', he wrote, 'its only drawback being that the French had a nasty habit of trying to get rid of dead mules by pushing them into the water. They didn't always want to go and sometimes loitered about for days.' Attached to this diary is a poem, A. P. Herbert's 'Helles Hotel', which includes the line 'And in their bathing place no mules decayed'.[2] The diary describes another role of the ubiquitous corpses in the trenches of Gallipoli. The author refers to the Turks by the all-purpose epithet for his enemies – Johnnies.

> Further inland, conditions were not so nice. In fact in places they were distinctly nasty, by reason of the fact that when Johnny built these trenches (they were his originally) he was apparently short of sandbags, so he had a little habit of working in deceased Johnnies here and there instead . . . they were apt to make their presence felt in a way which no self-respecting sandbag should do.

Willis Brown's unit was part of the Royal Naval Division Engineering detachment in Gallipoli. *With the RNDE* gives a very detailed account of the experiences of No. 2 Field Company there. Members of the unit were drawn largely from engineering and technical societies, complemented by a number of tradesmen, such as bricklayers, joiners, blacksmiths and navvies, many of whom had previously been constructing the London Underground. Many of the sappers had been at the public schools and universities. They embarked, minus the very ill Willis Brown, on HM transport ship *Somali* for the Dardanelles on 1 March. On 16

March they arrived at Mudros Harbour. 'The next day we were served out with pith helmets and we crowded on deck as we proceeded along the coast of Gallipoli.' They were not part of the landings on 25 April, but they received news that '50,000 men had landed on Gallipoli; with 3,000 casualties'.

They themselves landed on 29 April, in boats manned by sailors who 'told the most harrowing stories of what was going on ashore'. They slept in holes in the ground 'with the noise of battle on one side of us blending with the sound of the surf only a few yards away'. The next day 'our task was to make a road, a zigzag one wide enough for a field gun, extending from the beach to the top of the hill. We worked hard and finished the job, and amid cheers a gun was pulled to the top of the hill.' They were then taken off Anzac, and landed again at W Beach on 2 May. Here they were greeted by the sight of Turkish-dug 'mantraps', 'consisting of a large hole in the ground with wooden spikes sticking up from the bottom, the top having been camouflaged with foliage'. One of these had been converted into a mass grave for eighty-two NCOs and men of the Lancashire Fusiliers.

By 6 May the RNDE were participating in the Second Battle of Krithia, going 'over the top' of a trench for the first time. 'Laden with rifles, picks, shovels and other bits of equipment, we jangled our way across the open', sustaining several casualties. Their HQ was nicknamed 'Walmer Castle', after their training base camp at Deal; another favoured nickname of the encounter was 'Asiatic Annie', the legendary Turkish gun in the hills on the far side of the straits. The story continued:

Walmer Castle was often strafed by Asiatic Annie but there were so many dud shells that we became careless. We could see the flash of the gun and used to count up the seconds before the shell arrived. On Sunday June 13th we were having breakfast when a shell, that was not a dud, knocked two or three dug-outs into one. Worlledge, Kirkby, Astley and I

were involved and the sensation of being blown up was not as
I had imagined. I was very gently lifted up and dropped on to
my side and the only pain experienced was due to hot tea
which upset down the front of me. There were no casualties
but Astley was rather badly shaken. He seemed to worry about
this and a few days later asked, in all seriousness, if I thought he
was quite sane.

With the RNDE gives a description of a battle, the Third Battle
of Krithia, on 4 June, providing the context of Willis Brown's
breakdown and amnesia. 'The RNDE's task had been to cut saps
towards the Turks, for the machine gunners to use to get out of
the trench. A bombardment of the enemy trenches began, with
artillery and naval guns in action. The Turks retaliated. The
Hood, Nelson and Collingwood battalions went over.' 'We now
know' it continued,

> that they were enfiladed from the right where the French
> were supposed to have advanced. All we knew on that day
> was that there had been a hell of a mix-up, with bullets flying
> in all directions and our troops being shot to bits. Some of
> them came back towards our trenches and then turned round
> and went out again to what must have been certain death.
> Trotman's Road became crowded with the wounded and at
> about 3pm the sappers were told to go, so we made our way
> to the nearest communication trench. It took an hour to get
> there, and it was a ghastly journey with the wounded and
> dying around us. There were stretchers on the parados of
> Trotman's Road and although the occupants were presum-
> ably dead when put up there, the thought that they were so
> completely exposed was revolting. There was an incessant hail
> of bullets whizzing across the top of that trench.

After the battle the RNDE sappers were given the job of
altering an old Turkish communication trench. They had to

crawl along it, deepen it and begin a sap, not knowing quite where the Turks were. In the event, the Turks they encountered were mostly dead ones. On 6 June a small party of sappers went up to a trench newly captured by the Manchester Territorials. 'They seemed happy and bright despite the fact that there were dead and dying Turks around. Two of the boys were actually sitting on the back of a dead Turk, having tea.' Early in July there was another action, another batch of casualties. The RNDE sappers had to replace a trench that had become literally filled with the dead of a Scottish regiment. 'They wore kilts and lay there at all angles, their bodies swollen and almost black. From this heap of corpses came strange noises, as if some were alive and groaning, but the sounds we heard were due to the gases formed in those dead bodies as they decomposed.'

Willis Brown's experiences in the Dardanelles campaign were crystallized in the image of the trench of dead Turks. Accounts of Gallipoli invariably dwell on the corpses. The corpses were often so decomposed that they could not easily be lifted, and remains were put into large pits in the ground.

Willis, meanwhile, had been moved to the Naval Hospital at Portland. His mother seemed to have learned her lesson, as he eventually returned home and recuperated with no eventful moments. From there he got better, and applied for a commission in the Royal Field Artillery (RFA). On 17 July 1916 he re-enlisted and went to train for his role as a lieutenant in the RFA. Willis's RFA training was in England and when he could he got up to London to see his sister, who was learning naval camouflage at Burlington House, and living in a studio in Chelsea. They used to have lunch together from time to time, and take in a theatre show in the evenings.

As a child, Willis had always been prone to illness and accidents. According to his sister,

He inevitably caught everything that was going round, such as scarlet fever, which I never had. And where he fell there was sure to be a broken bottle, stray balls always found some vulnerable part of his anatomy, in a fight it was always *he* who got the black eye and *his* bones got broken when others received no harm. He seemed somehow fated to a succession of physical disasters and he would never admit that anything hurt. He would sit, grinning foolishly, and make some idiotic joke about it, so that people felt cross with him instead of sympathetic.

Willis took this physical vulnerability with him when he was posted abroad, and collected a large variety of health misfortunes.

He was sent with some guns to Salonika which he didn't like at all and where he got Malaria; and from there to the Suez Canal (sand-fly and dengue fevers) and at last into Palestine which promised to be interesting and exciting and even victorious for a change. But soon enough there came a letter to say that he was in an isolation hospital because he had been found to be a carrier of diphtheria . . .

By the late summer of 1918 he was thoroughly run-down. Visiting his sister in Cornwall he collapsed, shivering and numb. The doctor prescribed rest in hospital and 'no more War' but he ended up in the Army of Occupation on the Rhine.

By the end of the war, Willis Brown was exhausted. He was demobilized in 1919 without having any idea of what work he wanted to do. His father was 'mystified by the complete absence in him of any interest in his own future'. Mr Brown senior was perplexed that his son, now free to embark on a new life, had no motivation for anything. His father decided that a few years at Cambridge, reading engineering, might 'give him a chance to pull himself together'. At Cambridge, Willis managed to work hard enough to pass his exams, but he presented himself in the family as not taking his work at all seriously. He would tell his father he had no time for work, as cricket and bridge were so time-consuming. His mother was despairing of the two of them: 'father ought to have learnt to recognize his silly words by this time, but really Willis can be *very* aggravating'. His sister thought that it was just another symptom of his exhaustion: 'He hadn't the energy left to appear to be taking anything seriously and he could only cope with the years he had never expected to see by making a gentle mockery of everything, which anyway only had a slight and relative seriousness after everything he had been through.'

Over the years Willis seemed to recover his health. He played football, tennis and golf and even became a Territorial. He went to work at Hadfields, a large steel manufacturer based in Sheffield, and was eventually sent to Newcastle. In Newcastle he met the woman who was to become his first wife. This marriage had a most unpropitious beginning, as indeed did his second marriage. The first his parents heard about this relationship was that Willis was ill, that the doctor in Newcastle said he had to go home to be nursed, and that he was too ill to go alone. He arrived by car with a 'Miss Proctor', who stayed one night and then returned to Newcastle. Taxed by his mother on the topic of Miss Proctor, Willis said she was his 'dancing partner'. Mrs Brown was apparently uneasy about this, but after talking it over with her husband decided they were just being a little old-fashioned.

About a year later it transpired that Willis and 'Miss Proctor' had been secretly married for some months and that she was expecting a baby. Mr and Mrs Brown were horrified and immediately went up to Newcastle to look into things. They went first to the registry office to confirm the dates, to check that the marriage had not been precipitated by the pregnancy. Then they looked up Ethel Proctor's father. Apparently his wife had died of galloping TB after the birth of their second child and he could not cope with his two wild and unruly daughters. Mrs Brown quite liked Mr Proctor, but she had three reasons for being critical of the marriage. The first was that she despised Ethel's father for allowing her to marry a man whose parents he knew nothing about. Secondly, she considered the whole business rather furtive and dishonourable. Thirdly, as a great believer in heredity, she was worried by 'that TB in the background'.

Mrs Brown set about trying to make Willis's marriage more respectable. She insisted that the couple married again, 'properly', in church; it was decided they should move back to Sheffield where Willis would be found a more responsible and better-paid job. Willis and Ethel settled in Sheffield and the baby, Anne, was born. 'They adored her, and she brought out the very best in both of them.' Aside from baby Anne, things were not going well. Ethel missed her friends, and her sister, and did not like the move away from Newcastle; she would not engage at all with Willis's family and refused to return their social calls.

In 1927 their second child, David, was born. Ethel had returned to Newcastle for the birth, but shortly afterwards she became acutely ill and died. It turned out later that, exactly like her mother, she had died of galloping TB after the birth of a second child. Willis's sister Margaret went to help. They collected the baby from the relative who had been looking after him and set off back to Sheffield. Willis was 'distraught' with grief and shock. Margaret installed a nurse to look after the baby and returned to her own family. 'It didn't seem possible', she wrote, 'to do anything for Willis. He had retreated into a shell of despair where he was inaccessible and Anne was the only person whose voice he could hear. She slept in his room and mostly, I think, in his bed.'

A month or two later, Willis went with Anne to visit Margaret, then living in a place of 'peace and beauty' in Sussex, and he began to talk a bit. He told her that he didn't think he could bear Sheffield and Hadfields any longer, and that he was considering becoming a schoolmaster. She recalled that he went so far as to look at particular schools, before he was talked out of

it. 'The responsibility for two young children was too great.'
Much worse, he was to become dependent on his parents in a
new way. Within months of Ethel's death, the letters from
creditors rolled in. It transpired that she had racked up large
bills, using the name of her father-in-law to obtain credit. There
were huge bills for clothes, for food, for furniture. Willis was
appalled, having thought that his late wife had been a clever
household manager. He was doubly crushed, by the humiliation
of his household bills going to his father, and by the knowledge
that Ethel had kept that horrible secret from him.

Ethel's position had been made worse by the constant com-
parison between her position and that of Helen, the wife of
Willis's brother Malcolm. Helen came from a wealthy family and
moved in 'the best circles', and Ethel put a great strain on herself
trying to keep up with Helen's domestic standards. Ethel had run
aground on the reef of class difference. As Margaret later put it,
'the difference in our upbringing and education made what must
have seemed to her an unbridgeable gap'. Willis's marriage had
fallen foul of his mother's intervention in moving them back to
Sheffield; had they stayed as a couple in Newcastle things might
have turned out differently.

Willis had to give up their own place and move in with his
parents, and Ethel's debts made him more dependent than ever.
For the sake of his children he tried to make life at the family
home viable, but he and his parents got on each other's nerves
and he minded being under their control. According to his sister,
'Willis's spirit was broken for years and when he did begin to
revive it was with the same old irritating way of laughing in all
the wrong places to cover up real pain.'

Five years later, Willis met another woman. 'Mops' seemed to
be the perfect second wife for a battered widower – she was
capable, fond of children, well bred and looked distinguished.
His mother, needless to say, loved her, thinking her the perfect
daughter-in-law. Willis had got 'sort of fond of her' and wanted a
home of his own, and so proposed marriage. Then, suddenly, he

fell madly in love with someone else. Once again, the family history reverberates with his parents' disapproval of his behaviour. They had thought his clandestine first marriage 'dishonourable', but this was much worse. His behaviour, they thought, was 'shameful, dishonourable and altogether contemptible'. Nevertheless, Willis managed to extricate himself from the sensible 'Mops' and announced his new engagement. Enid was full of vitality, uninhibited and adored him. That was just what he needed then, and it seems that Willis and Enid made a go of their marriage in the longer term too.

What of the effect of all this on the next generation? Willis had two children, Anne and David, from his first marriage, and he and Enid had another child, Michael. Eventually, Enid was to love her stepson David as much as she did her own son Michael; little is recorded of anyone's feelings for Anne. In the beginning, however, Enid found the role of stepmother a difficult one. Her sister-in-law later said that 'she really wanted to be a loving mother to you and Anne and did her best, which may not always, to begin with, have been a very wise and perspicacious best. I daresay she may sometimes have been impatient and uncomprehending.' There was a time, continued David's aunt, 'that I heard that you were an unhappy and misunderstood little boy and I longed to adopt you. I thought you the most appealing and enchanting little boy and I'm afraid I thought very little about how such a separation might affect Anne.' Margaret was dissuaded from the adoption plan, but the suggestion itself shows what we would now call a 'parenting deficit' in the Willis and Enid couple.

It was only after Willis's death in late 1962 that this story could be told. David was the instigator, wanting to know more about his mother (Ethel), and wanting to understand the limitations of his father. His aunt, Willis's sister Margaret, explained the history of 'your poor, pathetic mother'. David's questions to his aunt, following his father's death, triggered a powerful, and ambiguous, response.

Oh David, I loved getting your letter. It made me feel quite irrationally happy but very sad at the same time because to read that you are fonder of me than of your parents must mean that your childhood and youth were more lonely than I had realized and also that my dear brother Willis can never have been able to get as close to you as I am sure he must have wanted to be.

Margaret's account of her brother's failure as a father touched on the miserable life of his daughter Anne, as well as the unhappy childhood of his son David: 'I was distressed for you when we said goodbye to Anne, just a fortnight ago. I think I know what all her troubles have meant to you and how sad and deflated you felt.' Margaret's account lays the blame for Willis's emotional inadequacy, as a father, squarely on his experience at Gallipoli in 1915. Referring to the succession of illnesses he had in later life, she asserted that 'I have always been sure that they were all the effects of those horrible experiences in the first war, both physical and psychological. The more he tried to bury them the more they ate into him.'

These illnesses, we hear, made up 'the last sad years' of Willis's life. 'Years of illness and frustration of many kinds which made him, no doubt, more and more oyster-like and apparently thick-shelled.' Elsewhere in the document she acknowledged that the Willis so damaged by Gallipoli had a temperament that might predispose him to emotional illiteracy. The balance is finely drawn: 'He always was so inarticulate about himself, even as a child, and could never explain his feelings. I think he was so sensitive that he was afraid of emotions in himself or anyone else; and, heaven knows, he had plenty to shatter him in his life.'

The cause of Willis's damaged life, and its consequences for his relationship with his parents, his siblings and, more importantly, the damage that this in turn did to his children, were attributed to the horrors of Gallipoli. That defining moment – giving up in the trench full of dead Turks — is the centre of this family narrative. Did Willis Brown's experiences turn him towards pacifism? They did not. The boy who had tried to enlist underage sought a commission in an artillery regiment, the Royal Field Artillery, as soon as he recovered his health after Gallipoli; later, in the 1930s, he was to be found as a volunteer in the Territorial Army.

Captain Douglas Darling, MC
2nd Machine Gun Company
Canadian Expeditionary Force

Walter Douglas Darling was born in July 1887 in Aberdeen, the son of schoolmaster James Darling and his wife Margaret Alice. According to his family, he must have inherited some capacities from his scholarly father, as he could read by the age of 3. He trained as a solicitor, and he enjoyed getting some military experience with the Territorials of the South Wales Borderers. As a young man, Douglas Darling emigrated to Canada. He settled in the Kootenay district of British Columbia, where he had a ranch at Soda Creek. In wintertime he worked as a solicitor in Vancouver, but it was the ranching that he loved. When asked, on his attestation papers in 1915, 'What is your trade or calling?' he entered the word 'Rancher'. Soda Creek, British Columbia, where Darling ranched 105 acres, was a tiny settlement whose name came from the carbonate of lime in the creek bed. It was located in the upper canyon of the Fraser River, at the beginning of 650 kilometres of navigable river water to the north. Before the railway arrived in 1920, Soda Creek had been a Gold Rush transfer point, a terminus for sternwheelers transporting miners to the north.

On 29 May 1915, Douglas Darling went to the enlisting point at Vernon, British Columbia, having decided to fight for king, country and empire. The attestation oath required him to 'defend His Majesty, His Heirs and Successors, in Person, Crown and Dignity, against all enemies'. Darling signed on for one year, or for the duration of the war and another six months, as a member of the Canadian Over-Seas Expeditionary Force. He was 5 foot 8 inches tall, 37 inches around the chest, had brown hair and eyes, and was a Presbyterian. On 4 June he was declared fit, and by 14 July his declaration was certified by a magistrate.

On his attestation papers Douglas Darling gave as his next of kin his brother, W. M. Darling, of Airdrie (Lanarkshire) in Scotland. A mere ten years later, in 1925, this brother was to act in that role, in registering his brother's premature death, in Dartford, Kent, at the age of 38 years. Douglas Darling survived his war service, but he never recovered from it. Darling was typical of many who had emigrated, but who returned to fight with the troops of the UK's Dominions. He took part in the celebrated capture of Vimy Ridge, in April 1917, which became an important symbol of Canadian national identity. It was at Vimy that the four divisions of the Canadian Corps fought together, attacking as a single formation under the command of General Sir Julian H. G. Byng. Douglas Darling's part in this historic battle came when he was a lieutenant in the 2nd Canadian Machine Gun Company. For much of the attack he was in charge of his unit, and he was awarded the Military Cross for his conduct that day.

Darling had gone out to France in October 1916, having been in training in England, at Shorncliffe, near Folkestone in Kent. The war diary for the company records that he joined on the 10th. Two days later he was sent to the front line. On 12 October, a diary entry reads, 'Weather fine. Lieut. Ptolemy to hospital. C.H.Q. [Company Head Quarters] back to Contal-maison road. Lt. McLean and Section relieved by composite crews 2 of A section and 2 of D. Section under Lt. Darling.' Lieutenant Darling's feelings about this rapid encounter with the front line can be seen in a message sent to his company commander. He wrote a field message to Captain Stewart: 'I am somewhat shaken up after the shell fire we went through this afternoon, but can hold on all right for a day or two. Will you be good enough to send up some Players cigarettes and a bottle of whisky.' Darling recognized a link between the stress of the war and his pattern of smoking. In July 1917, complaining in a letter to his fiancée about a persistent cough, he admitted that it would 'never be any better till I stop smoking cigarettes, which will not be during the war'.

Douglas Darling met, when he was training at Folkestone, the girl he was later to marry. Known simply as 'Bee', her full name was Mabel Henriette Marie Elizabeth Twiss. Although Darling fell in love with her when they met, he had an uphill struggle to persuade her that a relationship between them was appropriate – he had been presented to her on his return from Canada as a brother. On 5 October 1916, on his way out to France, he wrote to Bee from Southampton. This charming letter tells her that he had bought himself a 'murderous-looking revolver' at the Army and Navy Stores in London, and that he was currently 'impressing the population of Southampton with my ferocious appearance'. 'I shall never forget the last few days', he told her, 'you have been very good and sweet to me'. He wished that they were not both 'so reticent', as otherwise they would know each other better. He ended by saying 'Forgive this disjointed letter – I am still somewhat excited. Good night, my darling sister, and God bless you. Fondest love to Mother, Your loving Douglas.' Darling asked Bee to 'cheer up as much as possible, and prepare to write me long letters'. This she evidently did, and in early December one such letter revealed that she had just refused an offer of marriage. Darling's reply to this news was eloquent and formal, and he even invited her to show his letter to Mother if she liked. Darling wrote 'you know how I love you', that 'it was horrible to hear of the offer', but good to hear of her refusal. He had 'nothing but love to offer', and until after the war his prospects were uncertain and not bright. He asked her to write and tell him how she felt, saying 'if it is fated that you shall never love me in the way I desire, I shall never cease to be a loving big brother to you'. He told her that she was 'the centre around which my dreams are built', and asked her to answer his question: 'have your feelings changed in the last three months, dear? Or am I still a much-loved brother, and no more? Tell me truly.'

The 'Mother' to whom he referred was Bee's mother, who was later to act as a witness at their wedding in early 1918, and was not in fact his own mother. There was a family connection, in that Douglas had an aunt, a Miss E. Rawson, who lived in Chiswick. She had been present at Bee's birth and registered it in Fulham in 1896; presumably she was Bee's mother's sister, as on the birth certificate Bee's mother's name is given as Mabel Atlanta Markham Twiss, 'formerly Rawson'. It appears that Douglas and Bee were some degree of cousins rather than brother and sister, and there was nothing to prevent their marriage.

Darling's very frequent and detailed letters to Bee from this period onwards have survived: as is usual for wartime corre-spondence, hers have not and we have to deduce what Bee wrote to him from his replies. The correspondence enables us to trace, through his very open letters to her, the increasing nervous strain caused by his military experiences. He found it increasingly hard to face the shelling. They became engaged when he was on leave in the UK in early 1917. Darling's letters to his new fiancée offer a careful – he always had security in mind – description of preparations for a very important military push, and they also indicate some of his feelings about his army experience. As the build-up continued for the Canadian attack at Vimy, Douglas Darling gave Bee a clear indication of how it was affecting him.

In early 1917 Darling was a lieutenant in a machine gun company. He was second in charge, and the commanding officer, a Captain Stewart, was often out or away, leaving Darling responsible. A typical day for the company was 5 February: 'Enemy quiet with less M.G. activity. We fire between 11–12 thousand rounds during each 24 hours on targets within enemy's lines.' On 7 February the diary records Lieutenant Darling as on leave – he was in England getting engaged. On his return, he was sent to school for further instruction. Later that year he was to write to Bee that he had been selected as a Lewis gun instructor: 'I am a very lucky man – before the last big attack . . . I was sent on a course, and now, on the eve of another, I get this job!'

Meanwhile preparations had been going ahead for some while for a big advance. Even today you can see at Vimy Ridge the extensive preparations that were made for several months before this important battle. The Canadians constructed underground chambers, and tunnels for the infantry to use to reduce their exposure on the battlefield. The area was supplied with water pipelines, electricity, a light railway and tramlines, robustly protected communication systems, command headquarters and dressing stations. The men were briefed in full, and the attacks were rehearsed. The commander, Sir Julian Byng, had learned from the miserable fate of advances on the Somme and elsewhere. The troops would not attack in line and in successive waves, but each platoon would go forward very fast, attacking resistance on all sides. Objectives were straightforward. The attack was protected by a preceding programme of artillery assaults on the enemy guns, ammunition dumps, supplies and trenches. Machine guns would be deployed extensively. The attack would be accompanied by a timed rolling barrage of heavy fire that would move forward a hundred yards every three minutes.

Darling's company was part of the steady increase of pressure. By 21 February the company was firing 15,000 rounds day and night, targeting dumps, roads, approaches. By 28 February they were firing over 25,000 rounds daily at such targets. Darling himself was often at HQ in this period, doing the statistics and calculations for the guns. By 8 March the company was reconnoitring, and getting instructions of the appropriate positions of their guns for the barrage that was to come. On 9 March they pinpointed locations for sixteen guns for barrage fire. On 14

March the battalion's machine-gunners were instructed in the ways of German machine guns, as they would be required to use them once they had captured ground in the offensive.

On 15 March the brigade 'stood to' for four hours in view of an expected attack. The record for 17 March shows a raid on the enemy trenches, with ten prisoners taken, and Darling's collea-gue Lieutenant McFarlane sent to hospital. During the next week the company continued its usual firing and watched two of their side's planes brought down by enemy action. By the end of March all sections were busy, overlooking equipment and loading machine gun belts. The battle for Vimy began on 9 April, and the preparations that had taken place throughout March were escalating. Douglas Darling, whilst being careful not to locate his physical whereabouts, was quite forthcoming to his fiancée about how the military situation was affecting his state of mind. In early March he wrote to her: 'when I wander through these beastly trenches, I think of you all the time – especially in dangerous spots, when I hide myself as tho' I were shielding *you* instead of my own carcase'. As the pitch of battle preparation intensified, Darling wrote more and more of the effect his experiences were having on his nerves: on 24 March, 'we expect to be relieved within a week – I shall be thankful, for my nerves are on the jump, and I've been in here too long'. By 27 March, 'I'm very tired and generally disgusted with the war – the eternal racket gets on my nerves. Hope to get a rest in two days more, and shall be thankful.'

The battle of Vimy Ridge is described in detail in the official history of the Canadian Expeditionary Force. In this account, historian G. W. L. Nicholson emphasized the important place of the machine gun companies:

Promptly at 5:30 on the morning of Easter Monday, 9 April, the attack on Vimy Ridge opened with the thunderous roar of the 983 guns and mortars supporting the Canadians. The main field artillery barrage was provided by one gun to every 25 yards of front. These guns, opening at zero hour, fired for three minutes on the enemy's foremost trenches at three rounds a minute, and then lifted 100 yards every three minutes, slowing their rate of fire to two rounds per minute. This was supplemented by 18–pounder standing barrages, 4.5–inch howitzer concentrations, barrages by heavy guns and howitzers, and the continuous fire of 150 machine-guns, creating a bullet-swept zone 400 yards ahead. This employment of machine-guns for barrage and supporting fire was on a scale unprecedented in military history. The total number of machine-guns under the Canadian Corps for the operation was 358. Each of the sixteen Canadian M.G. Companies and the four companies of the British 5th Division had 16 Vickers, and the 1st Canadian Motor Machine Gun Brigade had 38. These figures do not include the 'liberal' supply of Lewis guns with the infantry battalions. Other guns and mortars bombarded German battery positions and ammunition dumps with high explosive and gas shells, while some mortars laid smoke in front of Thélus and Hill 135. This great volume of fire neutralized a large proportion of the enemy's guns, and the response of the remainder to the frantic S.O.S. rocket signals from German front lines was weak and ineffective, the ill-directed counter-barrage falling well behind the attacking troops.[1]

The attack was extremely successful. Although it did not materially change the stalemate on the western front, it was nonetheless a very important victory, and one made all the more significant for the fact that the four divisions of Canada's Expeditionary Force were fighting alongside each other and were completely responsible for the battle. The official Canadian Archives account of the battle concludes:

While the Ridge would never fall again to the Germans, the victory was not the long-awaited western front breakthrough to end the war. For Canada, Vimy proved the mettle of her men, the value of preparation and what Canadians could achieve on the battlefield when they fought as a unit for a common cause.[2]

Douglas Darling was in the thick of the battle of 9 April. At one stage, as second in command of the Machine Gun Company, he was in charge while Captain Stewart was elsewhere. He had to assert his authority in a manner that gives an indication of the stress under which he was working. In a field message to Lieutenant Jenkyn, the copy of which was found among his papers, he wrote:

> you will kindly recognize the fact that I am in charge of the barrage guns, at present, and any communication must be addressed to me, and not to the section officers. The O[fficer C[ommanding] will be here within an hour – if you want to make arrangements you had better come down here. If you wish to send messages to him – send them direct – we have no spare runners here.

Of the battle itself, which involved 40,000 men, of whom over 3,000 were killed and over 7,000 wounded, Douglas Darling wrote to Bee at the time: 'I am all right – it has been a glorious day for the Canadians'. It was not until later in April that the strain on him was becoming apparent: on the 16th he wrote that 'my nerves are rather upset' and again, on the 19th, 'my nerves are bad'.

Two years later Douglas Darling revisited the battlefield at Vimy. Not yet demobilized, he was given the task of escorting Bishop Stringer of Yukon over the sites of the battles of Arras and Vimy Ridge. On 25 January 1919, he wrote a full description to Bee:

> We came upon that abomination of desolation – No Man's Land of 1916–17. It is much as I left it, only the rank grass has

overgrown the shell holes and barbed wire – but the holes and
wire are still there. Here and there small groups of Chinamen
were at work, salvaging sheet-iron and the like stuff – but the
debris of battle is still there. We found old bombs, trench
mortars, rifles of all patterns, all sorts of decayed and rusted war
material – and once we came upon the skull of a Fritz which
still grinned up at the light of day from the long grass; while a
jagged hole in the bone showed how quickly he had died.
The war is over, but there I saw an awful mess to be cleaned
up yet. I found the place where I fired my barrage on Easter
Monday, 1917; but night was falling, and I did not have time
to explore it thoroughly; we were tired, and glad to get back
on the road. I wish you were here, so that I could show it all to
you, tho' it is a saddening experience. As we walked 'home',
the silence was oppressive; it was the silence of death; and I
almost longed to hear the dull thunder of the guns again and
to see their red flashes, and the white flare lights that used to
float so continuously in the air over No Mans Land. In those
days, at least, there was action and work to be done; now all is
desolation and loneliness.

The next day he was still unable to shake off the feeling; he wrote
again, to say that 'the battlefield is rather depressing – the silence
and desolation are oppressive'.

After the battle of Vimy Ridge, in April 1917, Darling was
sent to the Machine Gun School at Camiens, on the northern
French coast. In early May he wrote to his aunt that he was
recovering. 'I am already much better in health, I can sleep at
nights and my nerves are steadier – I was pretty well shaken up by
the strain of March and April.' On 13 May he wrote to Bee: 'I
hate to think of leaving this quiet spot so soon, and going back
into that hell.' Darling was then posted back to his unit. While
Major Stewart was away, he was to be put in charge of the
company. The unit's diary recorded this handover on 20 May,
and at the end of that month Lieutenant W. Douglas Darling was

the one to sign off the official record of the month's action. Writing to Bee on the day that he took over, Darling was worried about his hair: 'It is falling out very badly, though I persist with the rum and castor oil. Will you love me', he asked, 'when I'm bald?'

June and July were a period when Darling struggled continually with his nerves. On 25 June he was in charge again, and had been shelled – 'I'm so tired and nervous', he wrote, asking Bee to 'pray for me all the time'. By the end of June he began to describe his nerves in terms of 'shell shock': 'I have been most miserably ill – came out of the line with a touch of fever and shell-shock (I think) and only tonight am I reasonably fit.' Bee must have pricked up her ears at that, as by the 4th of July he was trying to reassure her:

> Don't worry about my health. I am quite all right, but my nerves are getting worse – I mean I find it gets harder and harder to face the shells, and I have an inward struggle every time I start out for the line. However, let us hope that I shall not have so much line work to do now that I am second-in-command.

By 8 July, he said he was rather better, though still mentioning shell shock:

> I am almost all right again today, though I have been rather miserable for a couple of days – I have never been quite well since the last trip – I believe if I had gone out at the time, I should have been sent to the base with shell-shock. Then I did not like to leave the Company when the O[fficer] C[ommanding] was away. I think that I shall be all right now.

On 14 July he was shelled again, and the next day he admitted that: 'I do get so sick of it all . . . It is miserable never knowing what may happen next, and it gets on my nerves. I always feel as if I were on the verge of breaking down, but I never get really ill so that I could get a rest.' Darling was not a 'Boche-hater' at all. In the same month as he was trying to cope with his own experiences of being shelled, he commented that 'I can't see how the Germans can stand the continuous bombardments – it must be terrible on their side of the line.'

Darling concluded that however attractive he found the peace and quiet of the Machine Gun School at Camiens, he could not sit out indefinitely. At the end of July he wrote to Bee, courageously stating what he felt to be his duty, while juxtaposing it with the inevitable anxiety:

> I realize that I am wasting my time here, and that my duty lies with the Company, and not in a 'bomb-proof' job . . . I believe that some of the most terrible fighting of the war is about to take place, and I feel in a continual condition of holding my breath.

The company was having a hard time while Darling was away. On 18 August they suffered a heavy gas attack, which resulted in Major Stewart, a junior officer and seventeen of the other ranks being sent to hospital. Darling, however, was still safely back at the school, having been made adjutant there. At the end of August he was saddened by the death of a friend: 'His ranch is beside mine, and we were a great deal together – enlisted at the same time . . .' On 1 September 1917 Darling wrote to Bee, acknowledging frankly his loss of morale: 'even after such a long time out of the line I am very nervous, and I don't know why I should be . . . I have somehow lost confidence (what little I ever had) in my ability to keep my head'.

Darling was at that time fretting that he was not being promoted. He was hoping for a captaincy, and perhaps the role of adjutant at the Machine Gun School might have carried that rank. But, as he explained to Bee, 'You are right – an Adjutant is generally a Captain and sometimes a Major; but . . . this school is

not an established institution, and the staff are only borrowed
from different units, and take their rank from their standing in
these units.' It must be likely, however, that this nervous man
was being passed over in favour of more robust colleagues. His
company was heavily involved in the Battle of Passchendaele in
November 1917. Several of the junior officers were awarded
Military Crosses and promoted for their role in it, according to
the war diary of the unit. There is no reference to Darling in the
record at this point. Darling was still in the 'bomb-free' zone that
he had bravely hoped to come out of. Presumably those who
took the decisions felt that his nerves were not strong enough for
more dangerous action.

In early 1918 Douglas Darling finally got the leave he had
been hoping for, though not – as yet – the rank of captain that he
also wanted. On 9 February 1918, he and Bee were married, by
licence and according to the rites and ceremonies of the Catholic
Church at the Oratory in London. The marriage was a great
success, as his long and intimate letters to Bee from then on
indicate. In 1919 their son George was born, and later a
daughter, known like her mother as Bee.

Back in 1917 Bee had asked him what he planned for after the
war and he had at that stage replied, 'I have not yet decided.
Possibly the Army, possibly a country billet in England or
Scotland – as for Canada, I'm afraid that you ban that.' He
was evidently sorry that his new married life would rule out a
return to his ranching days in British Columbia. In one letter he
described himself as a 'natural homesteader' and said it was 'a
Western instinct, to covet wild land'. In November 1918, after
the Armistice, he told Bee of a dream he had, in which the two of
them were crossing the Fraser River in an Indian dugout canoe,
going back to his farm.

Captain Darling was demobilized in July 1919. According to
the medical examination conducted in the depot in Seaford,
Sussex, at that point, his physique was good and his general
health and physical condition were good. But after the war

Douglas Darling suffered from consistently poor health. In January 1919, still in the army, just after his visit to the battlefield at Vimy Ridge, he wrote to his wife: 'I'm tired out and feel as if I could sleep for a week. I feel feverish and have a headache, but the doc. says I have no temperature, and has given me some pills and told me to go to bed.' His symptoms were hard to pin down, but he could not settle. His 'health had been broken', according to his daughter. His son George later gave his papers to the Imperial War Museum, stating that the family believed Captain Darling had died of the effects of shell shock. He had worked for a while as a solicitor after the war but had not flourished. Thinking that fresh air might be good for him, the family set up a poultry farm in north-west Kent. We cannot be certain what killed this man at the age of 38. The family's account of shell shock has to be set in the context of a death certificate that gives meningitis and coma as the proximate cause of death.

In 1919 Douglas had written to his wife, saying that on all his leaves 'there was always the horrid thought of my return to France to mar our otherwise perfect happiness', adding that 'it will be so lovely' when they faced no prospect of parting. Sad it was, then, that this couple had so little time together before Douglas Darling's untimely death, in 1925, at the age of 38.

Bombardier Ronald Skirth
Royal Garrison Artillery

In 1958 Mr Ronald Skirth retired from his post as a secondary school teacher in the London Borough of Ealing, suffering from deafness. In assessing his case for early retirement, specialists referred him to the Armed Forces Pensions Department and he was awarded a generous War Disability Pension, for which he could have applied at least forty years previously. He had lost the hearing in his right ear from exposure to artillery noise. But during the course of the war he had become such a pacifist that he was not keen, when eventually demobilized, to benefit financially from his military service. Only on retirement was he willing to accept a pension based on war disability.

Ronald Skirth served through two important battles of the western front, Messines and Passchendaele, and in the campaign in North Italy. He had the rare distinction, as he wryly noted in his unpublished autobiography, of actually leaving the army at a lower rank than when he joined up. Given the rate of promotion in wartime, when rapid replacement of dead young officers was required, we would expect a bright, competent, conscientious corporal to go beyond his non-commissioned officer status. Ronald Skirth managed to lose his corporal's stripe in the same month as he arrived in France, in an incident that gives an early indication of what was to come in his military career.

In April 1917 Skirth was the man who calculated the trajectories of the guns for 239 Siege Battery of the Royal Garrison Artillery, stationed in France. He was trained for this job as he was good at maths. Laying in an accurate course for the guns, with the distances and angles calculated exactly and correctly, was his responsibility. One day a visiting staff officer, Pilkington, took him out on an exercise and asked him to provide the calculations to fire at a particular target in the distance. Skirth, who had a thoroughly Church of England upbringing in Bexhill-on-Sea, Sussex, demurred at using a church for artillery practice, opining that 'only the Germans destroy churches'. Mr Pilkington in turn accused him of being 'a bloody conchie' and reported him for 'insolence to a Commanding Officer'.

The following day the battery noticeboard displayed the following announcement: 'As from April 23rd 1917, Corporal Skirth, J. R., reverts to rank of Bombardier as a disciplinary measure.' Worse for Ronald Skirth than losing the corporal's stripe on his sleeve, his prestige and sixpence a day in pay, was another consequence: he was relegated to the foot of the leave rota. At this early stage in his army service Skirth showed an obstinate streak, verging on devious, that would later come to the fore. He may have been punished for military indiscipline, but he nonetheless succeeded in his personal objective: 'I am pleased to be able to record that contrary to Mr Pilkington's confidential report stating that the target had been obliterated, *I* know that not one shell fell within 250 yards of its target. My calculations must have been very inaccurate!'

Bombardier Skirth was later to suffer what he described as a mental breakdown. The first few months of 1918 are missing from his otherwise very detailed account of his war experiences, as he suffered a period of total amnesia. Painstakingly, he later worked out how he had been treated, for 'shell shock', after being moved to the Italian front. Skirth spent many of his retirement years writing, and rewriting, an autobiography based on his diaries and memorabilia from the war. Excluding the

volume devoted exclusively to personal and family matters, this
document is now held at the Imperial War Museum.

Ronald Skirth was a well-read man; like many other young
men of the time, his favourite poets were the English romantics,
Keats, Shelley and Byron. His own description of the landscape
of Italy is illustrated through an extract from Shelley's 'Lines
Written Among the Euganean Hills, North Italy', which – of
course – he had with him in his *Golden Treasury*. Skirth is a lively
narrator, with a perky use of dialogue and a good sense of timing.
In short he tells a good story. Frustratingly for the historian, he
discarded his original sources when he had finished the creative
work. His autobiography is based on a factual record that has
been worked up, almost turned into a novel. Certainly it reads as
a *Bildungsroman*; the young protagonist emerges transformed by
his experiences and decisively grown in moral stature. On the
important points for his story, Skirth employed a logic of strict
selection. The autobiography as a whole is chatty and at times
long-winded, but the account of his experiences on the western
front in 1917 is distilled in the telling of just two 'war stories', one
entitled 'Messines' and the other 'Passchendaele'. These two
exemplary short stories reveal to the reader the exact experiences
that were to cause his subsequent breakdown.

Skirth's first war story describes 8 June 1917, a day that
changed his life. He was 19 years old but, he records, 'my
adolescence ended that day. Henceforward I had to live and
think as an adult.' On that day Ronald Skirth was sent forward
on an expedition across the scene of the battle for Messines
Ridge, encountering at first hand the effects of the British action
on 7 June, in which nineteen underground mines had been
successfully detonated under the German front line, killing an
estimated 10,000 men. The mines were followed by an artillery
barrage, in which Skirth, as the layer of gun courses for a siege
battery, played a small part. Militarily, the operation was a
dramatic success, and the capture of Messines Ridge was an
inspiration for battles to come. The new 'creeping' tactic for the

barrage had worked well, as it had at Vimy in April. The success of the mines has become legendary; at the time there was much comment on the fact that the noise of sending up one million pounds of explosive, 130 miles away in Flanders, could be clearly heard at 7 a.m. in London. Aside from the men killed, another 7,000 Germans, many of them dazed, were taken prisoner. Ron Skirth's experience that day, of seeing what had been done to the German forces, would change his attitude to the war, and him, for ever. 'War for me changed from being an abstraction to a personal problem. From that day forward it became MY war. *I*, not others, was responsible. *I*, not others, would have to live my life with a troubled conscience.'

On 8 June, a party of four men from the battery – Lieutenant Hedges in command, Skirth, his two friends in the ranks Bill and Geordie, and a carrier pigeon in a basket – were sent forward. Skirth was never told the purpose of the mission. Mr Hedges knew, but the party was subjected to shellfire and shrapnel, and he was knocked out fairly early on. Next came the deaths of Bill and Geordie, and finally, as Skirth thought to send a message by pigeon, he discovered he had been carrying a dead one around for some time.

What had the teenage Ronald Skirth seen that day? As the only survivor of a party of four we might expect a sense of danger to be the main feature of his account. But no, it is the physical revulsion of the dead bodies that permeates the 'story' of Messines. 'I can't attempt to describe what shapes and colours, things which were once human bodies and parts of human bodies assume after they have been blown sky-high. Some looked like bluish green replicas of the Michelin Tyre-men in the old advertisements – only inflated to twice *life*-size.'

Skirth's narrative continues:

Hedges, with his fingers to his nose, stumbled through and over these objects. I did the same, – for a short distance, then nausea overcame me. I had never set eyes on even a *peacefully*

dead person before. I cannot hope to convey to any one the
shock resulting from what I saw then. I had the utmost
difficulty in forcing myself forward, – over and between what
lay there. But Hedges was yelling like a man possessed and I
made myself follow. I turned my head to see where my two
pals were. One was being violently sick. As far as I could see,
ahead, to left and right we were the only living creatures in
that nightmarish landscape.

In the scatter bombardment that followed, Mr Hedges was hit,
and Skirth's friends from his unit, Bill and Geordie, were killed.
Looking for Mr Hedges, Skirth refers to the dead bodies as
unspecifiable 'things': 'There were hideous things to be seen –
but none of them were Mr Hedges.' With Bill and Geordie it
was different: 'I *did* find them. And how I wished I hadn't.'
Minutes later, Ron Skirth found a biblical sentence coming into
his head – 'And in death they were not divided'. 'How ludi-
crously inapt a quotation it was! For in truth they had been most
grotesquely and obscenely divided . . .'
     The 8th of June 1917 was for the young Ronald Skirth a truly
dreadful day. He survived a bombardment that killed the others
he was with, two of whom were his close friends, and he was left
in charge of an expedition with no idea what its object was. But
the appearance of the German corpses, blown apart by the mines,
dominates his account of the day, rather than the physical danger
he was in at the time. It is understandable that he should have
been so shocked by the dismembered, mutilated, inflated corpses
he saw that day. But the most lasting impression of the battlefield
the day after the capture of Messines Ridge was not, for Skirth,
those sights, shocking as they were to him. The emotional crux
of the Messines 'war story' was a very different corpse. Skirth's
reaction to it was very different too – instead of avoiding it he felt
'a compulsion to look which I could not resist', and as he
approached it he had to 'fight an inclination to faint' rather
than feeling nauseous or vomiting.

From the outset, Skirth used the pronoun 'he' rather than 'it'; this was not a corpse but a recently dead human being. 'Resting his body on the edge of a smaller shell-hole he had leaned back against a mound of thrown-up earth.' You would have thought, he continued, that he had assumed that position quite deliberately and just fallen asleep there. His posture was perfectly natural and normal, other than a felt, rather than seen, aura of death around him. The soldier's shockingly pale face was revealed by his helmet being tilted upwards, and a lock of blond hair was resting on his forehead. 'I thought Germans wore their hair closely cropped, – but not this one.'

Skirth was struck by how young the German soldier was. 'He was, or had been, no man. He was a *boy* who, but for the colour of his hair and uniform, must have looked very like me. I was nineteen, he probably younger still.' The boy had died looking at the photos in his wallet, one obviously of his parents, another of a young girl 'who could have been taken for Ella's twin sister'. Ron Skirth's story was from start to finish a love story written for his then girlfriend, Ella, later his wife, and his identification – through the image of their girlfriends – with the German boy was extreme. She had inscribed the photo 'Mein Hans', and the fact that Ron got to know the name of the German soldier was important – he later used 'Hans' as a shorthand for the unspeakable cruelty of war. 'What can he possibly have done to deserve *this*?' he wondered.

Ron deduced, from the fact that there were no injuries, that it could not have been one of the British mines that had killed Hans – 'it couldn't have been one of our mines, – otherwise his body would have been inflated till it had burst open to look like those . . . those other things . . . No,' he concluded, 'he must have died of shell-shock.' For Ron Skirth, this knowledge was tormenting, and his diagnosis of 'shell-shock' was troubling. He himself had been helping to fire the shells that followed the British mine explosions.

Hans had died as uselessly as Bill and Geordie. And when the thought came to me, as it did, that it *might* have been the blast from one of our shells, one of *my* shells which killed young Hans, I felt a sense of guilt almost overshadowing my pity and sorrow.

Skirth's account of this particular corpse clearly describes what was known as 'fatal shell shock'. Other and more scientific observers, such as Dr William Tyrrell, regimental medical officer with the Lancashire Fusiliers, noticed exactly the same thing in the aftermath at Messines – dead Germans with not a mark on them to show what they had died of. Tyrrell also attributed these deaths to 'shell-shock', however contentious that label subsequently became.

Ronald Skirth's reaction to what he saw at Messines was a decisive one – it set him on the road to becoming a pacifist. The strong empathy that he felt with the German boy had the immediate effect of destroying the idea of 'the enemy'. 'He *had been* my enemy, perhaps, but he wasn't *now*.' The deaths of his friends Bill and Geordie did not fire him up with hatred against the Germans, or make him want to seek revenge. Like Wilfred Owen, he saw instead a compelling vision of brotherhood: 'I am the enemy you killed, my friend'.[1]

Skirth's experiences at Messines, in June 1917, took place within a couple of months of his arrival in France. By late autumn his unit had inched further east and he was to choose for his second 'war story' an incident in the battle of Passchendaele. Whilst Messines was a triumph of British initiative, the battle of Third Ypres, running from the end of July to the beginning of September and popularly known as Passchendaele, carried some of the worst losses (the British lost at least 35,000 men) and the waterlogged conditions under which it was fought were appalling. Passchendaele is a small village just east of the Belgian town of Ieper (then Ypres) and General Haig had identified it as one of the first objectives of the advance.

Ron Skirth's account of 'Passchendaele' began in November 1917, when the battle had been going on for some months. He commented on the 'unending shell-holes nearly all containing horrific things that had once been parts of men and animals' and the 'ghastly horror of the sights and smells we had to live with'. In his physical description of the battlefield, he used the vocabulary of madness, of desertion, and of shell shock. At this point it was not him who was going mad. 'I am still amazed', he wrote later, 'that I was able to endure them [the sights and smells] for so long without losing my reason.' The person who *had* gone mad was, unfortunately, his commanding officer. Major Snow played a big part in Ronald Skirth's vexed war career and he absolutely loathed him. Snow was a regular, career, army officer and Skirth a teenage volunteer with sensibilities. Their mutual and increasing dislike was set against a background in which one eloquent fact speaks loudly: of the 120 men who made up the complement of the siege battery when Skirth joined, by the date of the Armistice he and Snow were the only two to have survived.

Skirth and his friend Jock were posted in a tiny pill-box, under the immediate eye of Major Snow. Skirth, however, managed to make his way to a nearby post where he discovered that – so untenable had their position become – the order had been given for a retreat. Relieved beyond measure, he went back, only to discover that Major Snow had torn up the order to retreat and was determined to make them stay forward. 'We had a raving lunatic in charge', wrote Skirth, variously describing Snow at this point as a man who had 'taken leave of his senses', as a 'madman' and a 'mad tyrant'.

Skirth took a huge risk and decided to retreat anyway, a decision which he knew could result in his execution. 'Desperation, or near madness dispelled all my fear of the madman I was facing.' He stood up to Major Snow and, taking Jock with him, went back, in disobedience to the orders of his superior officer. His description of their retreat, slithering from one duckboard to the next, fighting mud so deep that men, mules and machinery

simply disappeared in it, is very tense. In spite of the fact that they
were in extreme danger, Skirth was always aware of the corpses
around him and how nauseating he found them. In a rare
moment of irony, he pointed out that they only missed sliding
into a shell-hole, with its predictable contents of rotting bodies,
by the carcasses of some mules that saved them from rolling over
the edge. Eventually they were hit by a shell: Jock was killed, but
Ronald Skirth was blown clear, out of the crater, and was
rescued.

Following this, Skirth had his first experience of amnesia. He
describes a 'twilight period', where there were lucid intervals
amid a general backdrop of 'trying to remember'. He could not
remember being rescued; or being brought to Abbeville, in
France; he could not remember the time from 6 November to
the present time of 10 December – he had lost five weeks. On
the other hand he could remember waking up, unable to see, and
panicking that he had been blinded; realizing that he had blood
dried on his legs, that it must be Jock's blood, and fainting;
shrapnel being taken out of his neck; being told that his cigarette
case had stopped a bullet to his chest.

Skirth's memory was affected, but patchily. The narrative
continues, more self-consciously than usual:

> My brain woke up and said 'Jock's dead. It's all your fault.
> You gave him a cigarette, remember? Oh God! I'll never be
> able to smoke a fag again without thinking of him. Why
> didn't I die too? Like Hans! Who the hell was Hans? I can't
> sort things out.'

Skirth was also aware that his amnesia could be part of a
psychological strategy to cope with the charge of insubordination. Not only did he feel guilty about Jock's death, he felt
extremely anxious about the possibility of being court-martialled
and shot. He found himself hoping that Major Snow, the only
witness to his refusal of orders, had died in that crazy last redoubt:

'Dead men tell no tales. But *if* he had survived and I was put on the carpet I must lose my memory. Yes! That was it. Shell blast did funny things to men. I can't remember a thing – after that direct hit.'

Shortly afterwards, Bombardier Skirth was marked A1 fit at a medical, and entrained for Italy. The British Expeditionary Force were to relieve the Italians after the Alpine front had been broken at the Battle of Caporetto. He celebrated his twentieth birthday on the train, and described in some detail a journey in wagons marked up for eight horses each, which carried forty men instead, taking over a week to get from Abbeville in Northern France to Verona. The official regimental history of the Royal Regiment of Artillery put a very positive gloss on this long and tiring trek: 'the British were on their way: a seven day journey of 1100 miles along the Riviera with plenty of halts was a tonic to the weary men after months in Flanders'.[2] Skirth didn't mention any casinos, but he did manage to jump out of the train at intervals and send postcards, addressed to Ella in 'Bexhill on Sea, Sussex, Blighty'. These arrived, and were kept and later pasted into his autobiography.

Arrived in Italy, Skirth was billeted at the Villa Martino, near Vicenza, where he tried to get away from his colleagues, seeking solitude: 'more than anything else I yearned for privacy . . . I was convinced that the only way I could work out what I might call my regeneration was to have opportunities for contemplation'. He broke this pattern on Christmas Day, 1917, when, for the first and last time, he got very drunk. The hangover 'worsened the effects of shell shock' and he had persistent headaches. At the end of 1917 there was a great relief. He was summoned to the CO's office, and of course feared that this was the consequence of his defiance at Passchendaele. The officer in charge, a Major Jordan, tore up the papers in front of him and put Skirth on light clerical duties, a most compassionate decision. But Skirth also learned that the hated Major Snow would be resuming command of the battery, being reorganized in Italy, in due course.

This takes us to the first week of January 1918, and the moment of what Ronald Skirth was later to call a 'mystic religious experience'. This event was the last thing of any importance he could recall before his breakdown, and it was to shape his future, his life, in fundamental ways. Billeted in a house in the village of San Martino in the Veneto, he decided to visit the church over the road. A staunch Anglican, he approached it with 'boyhood prejudices against Roman Catholic superstitions and Popery' in his mind. An imposing building for a small place, the church was highly ornamented and decorated. Skirth sat down in a chair in a side aisle, looking around at the votive candles, at the gilded images and statues – the Virgin Mary, the Ascension. Let us take up the story in his own words:

Suddenly came the sound of the door being opened from outside followed by the noise of booted feet walking on the stone floor. I turned and watched a soldierly figure, helmet in hand, stride towards the altar steps, kneel upon one and cross himself. He bowed his head as he prayed. He was wearing the green uniform of the Italian army, meticulous in his smartness. An officer, evidently.

Below the altar steps there was a railed flat tomb which from where I sat was somewhat obscured, and beyond it in a niche was a statue. The soldier rose from the steps, genuflected and then stopped in front of the sculptural figure. I saw him kneel again and pause, then taking two candles he fixed them on their brackets, lit them and dropped some coins into the nearby box. All the time he was completely unaware of my presence.

I followed him with my eyes as, his devotions completed, he walked back towards the entrance. Just before reaching it he halted, brought himself smartly to attention, looked upwards and gave a military salute, having done which he opened the door and quietly disappeared into the street.

Ronald Skirth got up to see who had been saluted. 'Who was there . . . in an empty church, that he could regard as an officer superior to himself?' The answer: 'Above the doorway suspended by bronze chains from the roof was a near life-sized oaken carving of Christ on the Cross.' Well, of course, this is a central point of shared faith between Anglicans and Roman Catholics. Skirth's description of the scene until this moment emphasized the genuflecting, the mariolatry, the iconography, the votive claims, the buying of grace for cash, that were indeed his 'boyhood prejudices' about Roman Catholicism; here in the simple image of the Crucifixion there was no apparent distinction between the doctrines of the two churches. In any case, he was profoundly moved by what he had witnessed. 'The soldier's acts of humility and dignified piety affected me more than I can say. I had come into a Roman church ready to sneer . . . Yes, like someone in a quotation I only vaguely remember, I came to scoff and remained to pray.'

This was by no means all. Skirth then went over to look at the tomb, to see whose it was. It was a knight in armour, predictably enough. 'But this knight was an unorthodox character. He was holding his sculptured sword the wrong way round, its broken blade in his hand and hilt lying across his chest. The weapon of war had been transformed into the cross of Christianity.' Ronald Skirth then discovered that the tomb was that of San Martino himself. His Latin was good enough to translate the simple inscription, 'Blessed are the Peacemakers'. 'Of course! How dense I had been!' Suddenly, everything became clear to him: 'This was where his remains lay, – this was his shrine. This magnificently decorated church had been erected in *his* memory as well as to the glory of God, and the village which had grown up outside had taken his name.'

It was only later that Ronald Skirth found out what St Martin had done, which makes what happened next rather extraordinary. Had he known then what he subsequently found out, that St Martin had been a soldier who had renounced war when 'it was revealed to him that killing, even in battle was in the eyes of God sinful', what he did would have been explicable. But he did not know about St Martin at this point, which is why he describes the experience as a 'mystical' one. For what he did next was this: 'Then I made my vow. This is what I had really come for. I vowed to God that in return of his gift of life to me I would never, never knowingly, again help to take a human life.'

Ronald Skirth was serving in an artillery regiment at a time when the battle to defend the Italian front was about to go into a very active and important phase – his vow was going to be extremely difficult to keep. The story of how he managed to do so is an incredible tale of passive resistance, breathtaking in its audacity in relation to army discipline. He described the moment of the vow as 'the turning point in my young life': he had reached the end of disillusion, he had started to take the road back; he was embarking on his rehabilitation. In the meantime, he was heading for a mental breakdown. Shortly after this experience at the shrine of San Martino, he had to have treatment in the hospital at Vicenza – the shrapnel wounds in his neck had become badly infected. Prosaically, but perhaps symbolically too, these wounds had been festering and there developed an intolerable boil. As an unsympathetic doctor lanced it without warning, Ronald Skirth fainted – to regain consciousness three months later.

The 'lost months' from January to April 1918 were a great puzzle to Skirth, and it was many years before he was able to piece together what had happened to him. He knew he had two things wrong with him; 'shell shock' and a skin disease that was quite troubling. According to his daughter Jean, he suffered from psoriasis, a skin complaint which can have a psychosomatic dimension, for the rest of his life. But he had total amnesia as to what had happened after the episode in the Vicenza hospital. There were several distinct stages to his unravelling of the mystery. The first intimation of what had happened came quite soon afterwards, when he was acting in an independent role as a military observer. He wanted to buy a torch and decided to hitch, on his day off, to the nearby town of Schio. Skirth had been learning Italian and making friends locally, and he was given a lift by the postman, Luigi. At Schio Skirth had a powerful hallucination that he had been to the town before, and when he met up again with Luigi for the drive back he asked him about the place. The large building, Luigi said, was 'a big hospital for soldiers with "hurt heads"' – Skirth was convinced he must have been treated there, and indeed found that the building was called the Schio Hospital for Neurasthenics. Later on in 1918, Skirth struck up a friendship with an American Red Cross worker called Raymond, who actually remembered driving Skirth to the Schio Hospital to be admitted there. He also told him that a former colleague of his, then working as a Red Cross driver, had driven Skirth from Schio Hospital to the spa at Montegrotto.

The next clue came many years later. For the bulk of his war service, he had his detailed diaries, the cards and letters he had sent to Ella and which she had kept, and the souvenirs he had brought home. But for this period, January–April 1918, nothing. It was only after he retired that he decided to write up these contemporary sources into a discursive autobiography, and whenever he came to this 'lost' period he was stumped. However, a big clue appeared when he was, yet another time, rifling through his original materials – this would be around 1971. A flimsy piece of paper fell out of a book. On it was a crossword block containing apparently random letters, under which was written 'Ella holds the key'. Having encountered what was obviously a cipher, the elderly Mr Skirth set out to decode this message from his youth. 'I managed it fairly easily,' he said, as he assumed that he would have used the standard artillery code, and all he need was to find the code word – which was associated with Ella. He tried the name of her road and her second name with no success, but the message fell into sense when he used her surname. Given the religious experi-

ence he had recently had, this is perhaps no surprise: Ella's
maiden name was Christian.

The decoded cipher looks like this:

									1
H	Y	P	N	O	S	I	S		9
M	U	C	H	S	L	E	E	P	3
S	K	I	N	V	B	A	D		M
S	E	N	T	M	O	N	T		A
E	G	R	O	T	T	O			R
H	O	T	M	U	D	R	A	D	C
I	O	A	C	T	I	V	E	D	H
O	N	T	A	L	L	O	W	W	1
R	I	T	E	H	A	P	P	Y	8

In the right upright, framed by the year 1918, is the date, 3rd
March: this was Ella's birthday. The text reads:

Hypnosis/Much sleep/Skin v bad/Sent Montegrotto/Hot
mud radioactive/Don't allow write/Happy

It seems reasonable to interpret this as a private message to Ella
on her birthday. Not being allowed to write would explain the
absence of letters home from this time. A little more spec-
ulatively, it seems reasonable to deduce that Skirth was treated
at Schio Hospital for the 'shell shock', with hypnosis and sleep
therapy, and then sent to the Montegrotto mud spa for
treatment of his skin condition. Mr Skirth himself got information about the Montegrotto spa, which did indeed use
bathing in radioactive mud, still functioning when he was
writing, and a plausible treatment for psoriasis. More interesting perhaps is the treatment he received for 'shell shock'. All
we know is that he was in a hospital for neurasthenics in Schio,
and that he referred in the cipher to 'hypnosis' and 'much
sleep'.

With so little information on this crucial period, we must try and fill in the gaps as best we may, with informed speculation. Skirth wondered why he was handed over to the Italian psychiatric authorities rather than treated by the Royal Army Medical Corps, as would have been the case on the western front – perhaps because he broke down within two weeks of the British troops arriving in Italy, and arrangements were simply not in place. The British arrived in the wake of the disaster at Caporetto in October 1917. The Italians had repeatedly asked for artillery assistance from the British and French but it was only when the Austrians – using a spectacularly successful gas attack to open the mountain passes – invaded that the Allies agreed to reinforce Italy. After the defeat at Caporetto, many Italian soldiers were taken prisoner. In addition, an estimated 200,000 deserters scattered throughout the country. So there was at this time a large problem of rock-bottom morale, of failure of army discipline, and of widespread and shocking battle trauma. The gas attack, in particular, left deep psychological wounds.

The Italian scholar Bruna Bianchi has studied the military psychiatry operating in Italy at this point. As in Britain, there was some conflict between those who took a 'disciplinary' approach – emphasizing the problem of malingering and the need to return troops to the front, and often using quite brutal methods to do so – and those who were more liberal and sympathetic in their attitudes to war-weary soldiers with psychiatric troubles. There was one important difference, however: the Italian people did not support the war; it was imposed upon them. This meant that there was no hope of consensus, and it was known that elements of the army would be resistant.

The Italian military psychiatrists used a technical term for the soldiers who turned their incipient resistance first to a robot-like psychological dullness and then into depression and disorientation: 'depressive-soporose amentia'. 'Amentia' literally means the absence of mind, and is usually associated with extreme mental disability. In this context it was seen as a response to emotional trauma, and the liberal psychiatrists thought the cure was home leave rather than more discipline. Ronald Skirth was twice punished by having his home leave deferred, which meant that he served a year and a half with no home leave at all – an extraordinarily long period. In Treviso Hospital the diagnosis of 'amentia' was used in nearly 15 per cent of cases.

Bianchi points out that hypnotically induced sleep was particularly appropriate in the circumstances – soldiers were forced into automatic obedience and furthermore they were absolutely exhausted. So when it was 'suggested' to them under hypnosis that they should sleep, they did. One of the characteristics of the men who were treated for 'amentia' was a total dejection for which no solace could be found. Specifically – and here Ronald Skirth is a significant exception – they could find no comfort in religion, and lost their faith. Bianchi's study related to the hospitals of northern Italy in this period, and particularly the records at Treviso, near Schio where Skirth was treated. One marked feature noted in the Italian mental hospitals in this area is the following: 'even the peaceful reading of a book was disturbed by the appearance of images or the macabre shapes of the dead on the page'. These soldiers were often delirious, hallucinating and sleep-walking, trying to escape 'the spectacle of death'.[3]

Bianchi makes a distinction in her study between the case of officers and the case of 'men', and the pattern of amentia and depression she describes was characteristic of the ranking men. Officers were subject to more guilt and remorse for the deaths of men in their care. Ronald Skirth, as an NCO, regarded himself as neither an officer nor a 'man' in that sense. Skirth's experiences challenge the easy distinctions, made by academic commentators, between officers and men, just as he himself challenged the definition in quite deliberate ways. When he was eventually demobilized in January 1919, he travelled home by troop train from Italy. He took the stripes off the sleeves of his greatcoat, but left them on his uniform underneath so that

1. Charles Sims, *I am the Abyss and I am Light* (1928). Copyright © Tate Gallery, London, 2007.

2. William Orpen, *A Death Among the Wounded in the Snow* (1917–1918).
Copyright © Imperial War Museum, London, 2007.

3. William Orpen, *The Mad Woman of Douai* (1918). Copyright ©
Imperial War Museum, London, 2007.

4. Paul Nash, *Void* (1918). Copyright © National Gallery of Canada, Ottawa, 2007.

he could be a gunner when he chose, or he could take off his coat and be an NCO, 'choosing my rank to suit the prevailing circumstances'.

With hindsight, Skirth thought that guilt – presumably for the death of Jock, in particular – had been an important factor in his breakdown. Most of his memoir was written as an attempt at a faithful reconstruction of the period, but occasionally he reflected on these events from the standpoint of the present. Here is one such example: 'At the age of twenty I knew nothing of psychology – so how was I to understand that the cause of my mental malaise was my burying a sense of guilt deep in my subconscious where it was slowly poisoning my personality?' One officer in Bianchi's study expressed eloquently a position rather similar to the one Ronald Skirth eventually adopted as a consequence of his vow in the church of San Martino in January. 'I obey where I can, as I can, for as long as I am obliged to obey. Mine is, and will be for this whole period, a passive, inert, incomplete execution of my duty.'[4]

Meanwhile, the 20-year-old Ronald Skirth recovered: not his memory of the 'lost months', but his physical and mental strength, and he was sent back to his unit. But the vow he had made in the church at San Martino, just before his breakdown, was far from forgotten, and its consequences were very soon felt. On his return to duty, in April 1918, he was offered officer training. This was very tempting, mainly because it would happen in England, and would give him the home leave he had been deprived of for over a year. However, he declined. Ronald Skirth did not want any more responsibility for killing, nor did he want to benefit from it through promotion. But he really minded losing the time in England, and was very unhappy about the continuing separation from Ella.

Ronald and Ella's love story is a touching backdrop to his account of 'My War'. They met only three months before he enlisted, and she was fifteen and a half at the time. They were separated from April 1917, when he was sent out to France, until

December 1918, when he first got any home leave, after the Armistice. Given that six months was a typical tour of duty, he was certainly punished by an unbroken stretch of eighteen months on duty. During this period it seems that neither of them contemplated anything other than a future together; certainly neither of them appears to have so much as flirted with anyone else. Ronald tells quite a funny story about some colleagues trying, but failing, to get him into a brothel in Italy. Anyway, at this point, Ronald decided that he had to try and explain why he was acting this way.

He decided to clear his conscience. He would write to Ella explaining his new pacifist convictions, and the vow he had made in the church. As his letters were censored, this would reveal his attitude to his superior officers. He wanted to clarify whether or not the letter was allowed through; so he inserted this new credo as a postscript in a routine letter. As he thought likely, the postscript was removed by the censor and Ella received only the rest of the letter. The strategy had served its purpose: 'I wrote a declaration of my principles for my superiors to see.'

This 'confession' ran along the lines of explaining why he had just declined the offer of a commission, which would have brought him back to England. His feelings about the war had changed, he said, from what he had felt when he enlisted, believing it to be a 'just' war. 'I have become convinced that wars are wicked ways of settling disputes', he said, and that no one in authority was trying to stop it. He referred to 'fearful experiences' in Flanders, where he was nearly killed several times and said that 'the worst part was seeing my pals die'. 'Not long afterwards I had a mental illness. I had to go into a kind of hospital somewhere.' Next, he came to the part that was the hardest to say: 'Last Christmas I went into a church and I made a solemn promise . . . I vowed that because God had spared my life I would never help to take another's, – unless I had orders which I could find no way of evading.' As a consequence, he was faced with a 'terrible dilemma' – a conflict between 'my duty' as a soldier and 'my pact with God', 'my conscience'. He continued by saying that 'People who think like me (and unfortunately I've only met *one* who does –) are called Conscientious Objectors. To make it sound worse they call them Conchies. Nobody likes them.' He insisted that 'all the time I continue to wear the King's uniform I shall carry out the duties allotted to me as efficiently as I know how. No one will ever have reason to doubt my loyalty.'

Certainly, no one would have reason to doubt Ronald Skirth's integrity, but in the months that followed, the oath to God often seems to have won out over the duty to the army. He managed to find lots of ways of 'evading' orders he was not keen to implement. After refusing the officer training, he was appointed to an observation role. His task was to survey a stretch of the mountain front they would eventually move up to. The distance from the battery to the mountain front, where he had single-handed control of an observation post, took several hours to traverse, so he was given twenty-four hours on duty and then twenty-four hours off, a regime he loved as it gave him independence and free time. He was good at map-reading and other skills and made a great success of the survey. Skirth's observation post was basically a cave (he named it Cavella), traditionally used as a hermit's retreat and containing a small shrine, overlooking the gorge of the River Astico, running 3,000 feet below. On the other side of the gorge was the Austrian army, preparing to attack the British in the conflict that became known as the Battle of Asiago Plateau, in June 1918.

The terrain was particularly difficult for the artillery. The official history of this battle describes it thus:

> The British Artillery moved into the mountainous area south of Asiago, 23rd Divisional Artillery on the right and 48th on the left. [Skirth's siege battery was with the 48th.] The gun positions were all approached by steep slopes and hidden among trees; in most cases the guns had to be manhandled

into position and some had to be dismantled and carried up
piece by piece.[5]

Once up there, operations were difficult.

The Gunners found it extremely difficult to find gun positions
in the high precarious ledges which demanded large angles of
depression. In many cases the field guns, with their low
trajectories, could not clear the trees and 'lanes' had to be
cut for them. To hide the guns, saplings were lashed across the
lanes but the flash was still visible, so registration was usually
carried out by lone guns sent out onto the flanks. Eventually
reduced charges with improvised range tables were used. The
howitzers fared better but finding level platforms on the rocks
was not easy. Control of guns was not easy either since gun
platforms were often out of sight of each other. Commu-
nications remained vulnerable . . . Resupply too was a
problem . . . and much ammunition had to be dumped
forward. Strangely, water was scarce and had to be piped
from the Astico River. Daily maintenance was a problem,
with the wagon lines many difficult miles back.

All in all, a very inhospitable environment.

Ronald Skirth, meanwhile, had discovered something on his
survey. From his main post there was a tunnel to a second
observation post, and from there he could see something that he
knew would be regarded as a very desirable object for 'registering' the correct range of the heavy guns. This was an out-
standingly beautiful tiny chapel in the middle of the vista ahead.
In his actions to follow, we see the meaning of passive resistance.
He did not disobey any specific order, did not even have to
'evade' orders; but he patently acted outside and against the spirit
of his assignment. He took it upon himself to hide the existence
of the little church from his superior officers, in order to protect
it. He built a wall behind the shrine, to block off the position

from where the second post could be seen, covering his handi-work to form part of a makeshift sleeping area he had made up there himself. Calmly he noted

> I was confident that nobody other than the possible recluse . . . and the engineers who had originally excavated it, would ever suspect that behind that primitive façade was the blocked up entrance to a second Observation Post. I had made doubly sure by destroying the only map which showed its existence.

He was very proud of the fact that he succeeded in his objective, and after the battle the little chapel still stood.

Skirth's pact with God had not particularly tackled the pre-servation of churches; it had been about a refusal to take human life. Skirth now turned to the main point of his vow, which had direct implications in the days to follow. His scope for action was very much enhanced by the fact that his specific role was the laying of gun courses, the exact calculation of range and target. He decided to ensure that the Austrians were never taken completely by surprise.

> The nearest enemy hutments were a hundred yards away and I should arrange for my preliminary *mis*-calculations to ensure that the first shells we fired gave the Aussies adequate warning . . . Every time I took part in an 'action' from then till the war ended, I did the same, so that we never once hit an inhabited target, intentionally anyway, first time. Our first rounds always fell wide or short. I got great comfort from all this; feeling a sense of power that nothing else ever gave me. There was something quite unprincipled about this, of course, but as no one knew (apart from me and the Almighty, who I was confident looked the other way while all this was going on) I felt no sense of guilt whatever.

Ronald Skirth developed through these experiences a considerable confidence in himself. His religious experience had given him a basis for transcending the passivity now known to be an important element in 'shell shock' and the mental illnesses characteristic of trench warfare. The 'sense of power' he obtained from his strategy was a substantial one; he had successfully got around military authority and realized his own objective, at the age of 20 and holding a low rank. He had acquired the power of effective passive resistance; towards the end of his memoir he commented that there was 'more Christianity' in Gandhi than in the Archbishop of Canterbury.

The Battle of Asiago Plateau, which began in the early hours of 15 June, would crystallize his opposition to the values of the military professionals. When the bombardment began, at 3 a.m., Skirth was alone in his observation post. Not sure what to do, he became worried about the placement of one of the guns and decided to make his way there to try and prevent it being fired. He believed that its elevation was too low, but had not liked to challenge the sergeant whose responsibility that was. Unfortunately he was right, but the gun had just been fired – the shell instantly hit the rock face above and the team were injured and buried by falling rock. Skirth ran to the Italian First Aid Post at Fontanella, where a friend of his, Giulio, had an ambulance, as he knew this would be the quickest way of getting medical help. On the way to the hospital at Vicenza the ambulance took a direct shell hit, killing two of the wounded men. Giulio was slightly wounded; Skirth lost a lot of his hearing.

Ronald Skirth wrote a report on his actions following the 'premature shell burst', and took it to his commanding officers. When he arrived back at base, he found the hated Major Snow had returned to take charge. Instantly, Skirth was terrified that the Passchendaele insubordination was to finally catch up with him, but his bacon was saved by an extraordinary piece of luck – Major Snow was also shell-shocked and had amnesia. 'Do you know this man?' he asked the acting Officer Commanding, a Captain Hemming-Wale. Skirth's predominant feeling was huge relief at not being recognized. Snow's appearance shocked him: 'He looked quite twenty years older, very tired, haggard, emaciated; like a skeleton that had been thrust inside a shrivelled skin that was too small to hold it comfortably.' The fingers that picked up Skirth's report trembled and shook. Nevertheless, Snow's general personality seemed unchanged, and he put Skirth's report to the flame, saying 'There was no premature shell burst . . . The casualties were caused by enemy action.'

Only later was the motivation for this cover-up revealed – preferment. For their repulsion of a surprise attack by the Austrians, this battery were awarded several medals. Major Snow got a bar to his DSO and was promoted to the rank of lieutenant-colonel; Captain Hemming-Wale received the Military Cross. To Ronald Skirth, these were both entirely undeserved. Sergeant Waller, who died in the ambulance with Skirth, was awarded a posthumous Distinguished Conduct Medal, which Skirth hoped would be of some comfort to his family. Ronald Skirth himself was offered a Military Medal, but refused it, on the grounds that his religious beliefs precluded him from accepting rewards for killing people. This gesture earned him another relegation to the bottom of the leave rota. The medal, at Snow's disposal, then passed to the very man who had incompetently failed to elevate Gun No. 1 properly in the first place, Sergeant Bromley.

Skirth's response to this incident was not much tempered by the awareness that Snow was still suffering the effects of the shell shock that, by the coincidence that seemed to dog them, they had both been left with after Passchendaele: 'I judged him to be a sick man, but could feel no compassion towards him'. The naked self-interest that lay behind Snow's refusal to acknowledge a 'premature shell burst' was anathema to Skirth: 'This last example of the depths to which a senior regular soldier could sink in the pursuit of his ambition only added to a detestation which I had already found difficult to conceal.'

In October 1918 Ronald Skirth was part of the northward advance of the British troops in Italy, near Spresiano, which culminated in the Battle of the Piave. This, decisive in winning the war on this front, was shortly followed by the Armistice of November 1918. In December, Ronald Skirth was given ten days of home leave, and he was demobilized ten weeks later, in early 1919. Before he left Italy he decided, on one of his days off, to visit the battlefield of the River Piave.

> I thought that by now the horrors of war could no longer shock me. I was wrong. It must have been some ghoulish influence that drew me to the old battlefield and three months after the fighting had ceased the mangled, putrefying bodies of men and beasts still lay awaiting burial. I wished I hadn't gone.

On his last evening in Italy, in Treviso, he tried to weigh up his experiences there since St Martin had played an important part in 'my physical and spiritual redemption'.

> My thoughts strayed back over the past fourteen months, from the time of my arrival in Italy physically sick and on the brink of mental collapse, to the present day. If I excluded from these memories the ugliness and cruelty, the bloodshed and terror of the relatively few occasions when I had taken a part in actual battle, I could look upon the transference from Belgium to Italy as a transportation out of Hell and into Heaven. And tomorrow I was to leave healthier in body and spirit than I had ever been before.

Ronald Skirth and Ella Christian were married in 1924; they had one daughter, Jean. A trip to Italy was never possible on a schoolmaster's pay, but Ron maintained a lifetime ambition to return to the place whose beauty had played such a part in his mental salvation. The 'Retirement Gratuity' of a grateful nation made this possible when he retired. In 1961, forty-three years after he had left Italy, he and Ella had a second honeymoon, visiting the North Italian places that had made his sanity, and their life together, possible.

Air Vice-Marshal Sir William Tyrrell
KBE, DSO and bar, MC, MB, BCh, DPM

William Tyrrell began the war as an immensely likeable and popular chap. He went out to France with the British Expeditionary Force in August 1914, as the medical officer for the 2nd Battalion of the Lancashire Fusiliers. His correspondence is full of letters from men who were sure he had saved their lives. He also received enormous numbers of letters from wives, widows, sisters and girlfriends of men whom he had treated. Often Tyrrell wrote to these women when the men were wounded or killed – and many of these letters show profound gratitude to this very caring doctor and colleague.

William ('Billy') Tyrrell, born in 1898 the eldest of ten children, trained in medicine at Queen's University Belfast and distinguished himself as an athlete and international rugby star. Tyrrell came from an established Belfast family: his father was an alderman on Belfast City Council, and at one point high sheriff of the city. Young Billy followed in his father's footsteps, not least in becoming a Freemason. On 2 February 1914 'Bro Tyrrell' paid five Guineas for his 'Initiation' at Richmond Masonic Lodge No. 262 in Belfast. His father John was chosen, after the war, by Belfast 977 when the time came to unfurl a new memorial banner of the 36th Ulster Division. The local paper reported that 'the Lodge had been very fortunate in their choice of a gentleman to perform the unfurling ceremony.

Alderman Tyrrell's family had made a great sacrifice in the great war.'[1]

Among Tyrrell's qualities was that of being incapable of throwing anything away, and his voluminous papers contain mountains of ephemera from his wartime experiences. Tyrrell eventually became an expert on fear and morale and, in his capacity as medical director of the newly established Royal Air Force, he gave evidence to the Southborough Committee on shell shock. Typically, he admitted in his evidence to having given way to shell shock himself at one point, and it is his case that is written up in the final report as the anonymous witness of a 'gallant officer'.

William Tyrrell's experiences in the First World War certainly changed him. When he arrived with the Lancashire Fusiliers, according even to the regimental history of the war, 'he soon endeared himself to everybody'.[2] From being an enormously admired and popular chap – very 'clubbable' indeed – he ended up with a considerably authoritarian stance on questions of discipline. This evidently charming young man turned, in later life, into a man so conscious of rank and authority that he developed an odd habit. Before filing away letters he received, he added, in his own handwriting, the appropriate letters after the name of the person who had written to him. With doctors he would append their medical degrees and qualifications, and military men would get their decorations added; as he became more senior he would be able to add knighthoods and so forth.

In August 1914 Billy Tyrrell was a young doctor of 26. Having signed up on a reserve basis, he was immediately called up and sent to France and in later life he was proud to attend meetings of these original 'Old Contemptibles' who survived the war from its earliest days. In December 1914 he was decorated for bravery. The regimental history records the event:

On the night of 10th December, a man of the battalion who was on duty in an advanced listening post was severely wounded in the legs. Owing to the flooded condition of the trenches, it was impossible for the stretcher-bearers to carry him away in the usual manner. Tyrrell, the medical officer, who possessed the physical strength that might be expected from a former Irish Rugby international, went out and, with an entire disregard for his own safety, carried the man back to a point from which he could be taken on a stretcher. For this gallant action he was recommended for a very high honour: he was awarded the Military Cross in the first list of recipients of this newly created decoration.[3]

Touching as this story is, it is the first of numerous occasions when Tyrrell's success was for him tinged with a little resentment; he was actually recommended for a VC (note the 'entire disregard for his own safety'), which he did not get.

William Tyrrell in 1914 and 1915 was a young man yet to be brutalized by war, and he used his diary to express feelings that later he would suppress or be too busy to record. On Christmas Eve 1914 he confided that 'as usual on night we go into trenches I've got the needle – just the same before a big match and tonight I think I'm worse . . .' Later that evening, at 9.45 p.m. he endearingly wrote to his girlfriend: 'Goodnight May! Good night everybody at home.' At this early stage in the war we hear a certain amount about Billy Tyrrell's social activities. He records a little 'amateur cooking', making scrambled eggs all round in October 1914; in April 1915 he was captaining a rugby team for the 4th Division; there are many concert programmes recording his appearances as a baritone singer of songs such as 'Maire, My Girl'. When the peripatetic little church arrived with its pulpit and a small pedal organ, it was Lieutenant Tyrrell who played for the congregation.

In 1928 a memoir appeared in the *Journal of the Royal Army Medical Corps*, about an '*Entente Chirurgicale*' between the British RAMC in France and the French local people and staff. Tyrrell figures as 'Lieutenant William T. Raff' (the Raff came from his subsequent career in the Royal Air Force). The author conjures him up: 'Since those days William has risen to exalted rank and dizzy eminence; but in September, 1914, he was known as an international athlete, a good singer, a confirmed optimist and a great exponent of la joie de vivre. Naturally, William was a great favourite wherever he went.' He describes him riding horses at the depot of the local French cavalry regiment: 'As a broncho buster William scored an immediate and popular success.' The evenings were enlivened by 'a series of grands cours de l'Entente' in which 'our William again figured as a star performer'. This cameo of Tyrrell in the autumn of 1914 concludes with the claim that 'The exploits of "Le Chevalier Guillaume R-rraf" are enshrined now in the traditions of the Officer's Mess of the Lancers of Lorraine.'[4]

Meanwhile, there was the war. Tyrrell made a dramatic entry into the history books of military medicine in April 1915. Stories about the role of urine in protection against gas are often thought to be apocryphal; this one is recorded in some detail in the regimental history of the war, as well as in informal records among Tyrrell's own papers. The first German gas attack at Ypres was on 25 April 1915; this account starts at 4 p.m. on 2 May, when B Company of the 2nd Battalion of the Lancashire Fusiliers were having a cup of tea. A slight breeze was blowing from the east, when yellow clouds appeared, coming from jets put into the German lines at intervals of three or four to every hundred yards. The clouds then settled into 'thick, billowy waves about three feet high' which were rolling towards the British lines. These took three or four minutes to cross no-man's-land, and a general gas alarm was given. Assuming that an attack would follow behind the gas, positions were manned and fire opened with rifles and machine guns.

The main problem was physical gas protection.

Such men as had respirators put them on. These consisted of small rectangular pads of compressed cotton wool soaked in a solution of sodium hypochloride which had been issued at Vlamertinghe on a scale of two to each platoon . . . most of the signallers and machine-gunners . . . had none at all. But these pads were ineffective as they did not cover the nostrils . . . Fortunately, the medical officer remembered the fireman's trick of holding a wet cloth over the mouth and nose when fighting fumes, and proceeded to adapt it as best he could.

Less fortunately, the containers of water, and the tea they had just been drinking, were overturned in the alarm, and there was no suitable liquid to use. 'Following his example, however, all those within reach of his voice proceeded to wet their handkerchiefs or any handy piece of material with their urine and tie it over their face. This expedient proved very effective, especially as the natural ammonia helped to neutralize the chlorine in the gas.'

This measure was extraordinarily effective. B company, 'thus horribly protected', went on to defend the position. They saved the situation, 'but at what a cost!' Out of nearly 200 men, about thirty were fit for any kind of duty: 'the trenches and surrounding area, reeking with a sickly smell of chlorine, were littered with men already dead and others slowly and painfully dying of asphyxiation'. The report notes that 'it is significant that the only officers and men in the battalion who were able to carry on at the end of the day were those in "B" Company's sector who followed Tyrrell's advice.' It was found that 'there was a gaping hole in the line originally held by "A", "C" and "D" Companies'. Of these companies there were 'no signs beyond one man on the parapet, completely out of his mind, and three signallers in the headquarter dug-out badly gassed . . . It was only too clear that the greater part of the battalion was out of action.'[5] A force of 1,100 had been reduced to 88.

Another problem was the natural tendency of the men to run from the gas. As that inevitably meant running with it, the officers, including Tyrrell, rightly urged them to stay where they were and wait for it to pass over. Stories of Tyrrell's behaviour that day contributed to his growing reputation. One of the men described him later as 'more than a hero';[6] an officer subsequently commented that Tyrrell had done 'everything which a doctor shouldn't do as well as everything he should do'.[7] Apparently Tyrrell was so angry that he had picked up the rifles of dying men and fired at the Germans himself. In another story from that day, it was suggested that he had 'persuaded' men not to run from the gas by threatening to shoot them if they did, thus saving their lives.

From that time on, Tyrrell became more clearly an army officer as well as a doctor. Soon afterwards the acting adjutant, a Captain W. J. Rowley, was forced to go into hospital. Dr Tyrrell was appointed to fill this position for an interval, as well as holding down the job of a regimental medical officer. There was no incompatibility between his two roles. During one of his spells with this dual responsibility, there was an alarm that the enemy were mining under their section of the line. Divisional headquarters were asked for advice and sent the following message:

> Engineers are getting listening rod [stop] until it arrives they suggest sinking a bucket of thin tin box in ground and ramming earth tight all round [stop] fill it with water and either immerse one ear or better still borrow a binaural stethoscope from your adjutant and listen with its end in the water.[8]

Tyrrell was to face another episode with shockingly heavy casualties, less than two months after the gas attack in the Second Battle of Ypres. In July 1915 the battalion, though still sorely depleted from the events in May, was sent to relieve the forces who had recently taken a stretch of German trenches east of the Iser Canal, south west of Pilckem. The new position was very vulnerable to German counter-attack and was heavily shelled.

Tyrrell gives a gloomy list in his Boots pocket diary of the toll from 10 July, when apparently a shell hit their headquarters.

> Officers killed. 8
> Capt Smith
> Lt Simpson
> 2Lt Pickering N Staffs
> 2Lt Kelly
> 2Lt Billington
> 2Lt Brickell
> 2Lt Stanwell
> 2Lt Charleston D of wds
>
> Officers Wounded
> Col C J Griffin
> Capt Spooner
> Lt Appleby
> 2Lt Granger
> 2Lt Nairne since *dead*
> 2Lt Mson
> 2Lt Johnstone
> 2Lt MacIver
> 2Lt Wase-Rogers

Many of these names figure in Tyrrell's later correspondence: a friend of Lieutenant Nairne told him she would travel anywhere to meet him and talk to him about what happened. The First World War section of the history of the Lancashire Fusiliers, put together by J. C. Latter, relies in places on Tyrrell's own account, written in 1938, of what happened. Although the medical officer, he referred to 'isolated and brief incidents during which, through no virtue of mine, but owing to sheer force of circumstances ie enemy action and resultant casualties, I was left more or less single handed at Battalion Headquarters in virtual command of the situation'.[9]

Describing the aftermath of this particular battle, Tyrrell said that

> the Battalion, or what was left of them ie four or five officers
> and about 150 men were withdrawn to rest billets near Poven
> which was reached about dawn . . . As the shattered remnants
> of the Lancashire Fusiliers struggled into Poven, the troops
> already located there, aware of the grueling the Lancashire
> Fusiliers had had and how they had held the line, turned out
> in a spontaneous parade and paid the Lancashire Fusiliers the
> unique compliment of voluntarily presenting arms as the
> Lancashire Fusiliers marched past to their billets.[10]

For the rest of his life, Tyrrell would attend events connected with the regiment: he was present at the unveiling of their war memorial in Bury in 1922, a regular contributor to their benevolent funds, a keen attender at their reunions and dinners, and a lifelong friend of the wounded Captain Spooner.

By the end of July 1915, Tyrrell had seen the decimation of his battalion. 'Put in for leave,' he wrote in his diary, 'may get 7 days. Everyone good to this orphan nowadays.' At this point the focus was on how he coped with such high casualties. Also among his papers for this period is one little scrap with some significance for how he was later to understand psychological frailty in war. It is a flimsy note, obviously sent by runner: 'Dear Doc, Could you raise a bit of rum or other spirits for four stout fellows who have to dig out and re-inter a Frenchman very much decomposed, tonight? It's a beastly task and the poor devils deserve something and I haven't got a drop of anything. Yours, G.'

In the autumn of 1915 William Tyrrell was cracking up; it is the one period not well represented in the many boxes of his papers and souvenirs from the war. In 1922 he was asked to give expert advice to the official inquiry into 'shell shock' and in the written evidence he submitted to the committee he stated that shell shock was a condition to which 'I once temporarily gave

way myself'. His account at that point was that 'I was myself
thoroughly shell shocked. I was foolish for a week, but after six
months out of the turmoil I was perfectly well and returned to
the front and completed there the last two and a half years of the
war.' What he meant by 'foolish' and exactly where he was for
the next six months were not spelled out then. The committee,
however, asked if he would be willing to give, as an anonymous
witness, an account of what had triggered his shell shock, and this
he did.

Tyrrell began by describing the casualties in his battalion
during the three months of the Second Battle of Ypres, earlier
that summer. 'The personnel, officers and other ranks, changed, I
should say almost completely, four times. After the third time I
knew I was "for it". You can understand what I mean. I knew I
was approaching the end of my tether.' He was then sent home
on ten days' leave, to fit him for a big attack that was coming up,
and he spent it at home in Belfast and then in London where 'I
tasted life in practically every way that I could taste it . . . I did
not think I should have another chance.'

On his return, they attacked successfully, taking over German
trenches and occupying their supports and reserves. Effectively
this brought them into the German front line and their new
position was an easy target: 'they were able to enfilade our whole
position'. A German counter attack then took place, in which 'to
make a long story short, during the succeeding 48 hours the
battalion lost about 70 per cent of their personnel'. Tyrrell
described the counter-attack as 'the most terrific fire I had been
through during the war. I never had an experience to exceed it.'
They were sheltering in the German dugouts, which were
perfectly in range of the German guns. At one point a 5.9 shell
came right in, killing three and severely wounding another three.
Tyrrell himself knew his moustache, eyebrows and hair were
singed, but was otherwise 'visibly unhurt'. 'We got rid of the
wounded and the dead were pushed on one side, and we tried to
carry on . . .'

Their casualties were heavy, and those in the front line were heavy, and 'it became a question of holding on' as help was not at hand for some time. When it did arrive, 'my help personally came in the shape of two officers from another regiment. I knew then that my time had come absolutely. I knew as soon as they arrived that my time had come.' Tyrrell showed them the scene and then 'shrunk' into a deep dugout. 'Now I had time to think, I do not mind telling you, I was in absolute terror.' At this point he thought he was going mad – he would look at his watch, thinking hours had gone by, to discover that only seconds had in fact passed. 'I told myself that my brain was going.'

The dugout to which he had retreated was well made, with huge trees laid across its roof, which was just as well for Tyrrell as it then took a direct hit. He was saved by the breathing space afforded by the huge trees, and was eventually dug out by some stout fellows who came back for him an hour later. Meanwhile, he had been reported dead. Twenty four hours later they were relieved, and he said that some of the men coming in were in tears: 'the trenches were nothing but mud and blood. There was nothing to take over . . .' At this stage, Tyrrell again 'was all right and had good control of myself'. But the last straw was about to be laid on his back:

I was perfectly all right until what remained of the men, approximately 300, three young boys (officers) and myself were mustered behind the lines and proceeded to march out. Just about dawn we got back as far as where the quartermaster had come to meet us. He brought up all the officers' horses and there were no officers to ride them, and when I saw the horses and realised what had happened I broke down and I cried. That finished me.

Afterwards, Tyrrell had a week, in which 'I could not control my tears'. Also there were to be some 'nightmare and dreams' ahead. But after 'six months down the line' he was able to go back to the front and 'had no difficulty in controlling myself'. After these experiences, Tyrrell was posted 'down the line' to a less stressful environment. The repeated loss of friends and colleagues, the 'mud and blood' of the dead and wounded, the live burial, were all traumatic enough in themselves. To the committee he said, 'Well, I think that was "shell shock" I had. I lost control when I went into the dug-out and concealed myself . . .'[11]

This incident was in the autumn of 1915. Tyrrell was then sent back, leaving the Lancashire Fusiliers, to work at Static Hospital No. 4, considerably back behind the front lines. The organization of the Royal Army Medical Corps, from the front line moving backwards, during this period was :

Regimental aid posts
  (at the front)
Advanced dressing stations   } Field and motor Ambulances
Main dressing stations
Casualty clearing station

Stationary hospitals
Convalescent depot   } Ambulance trains
Base hospitals
Hospital ship

Putting Dr Tyrrell in a static (stationary) hospital removed him from imminent danger of bombardment and his own death, and winnowed out the gross surgery and dying patients who were not good for medical morale. This became an established practice, and Tyrrell himself, when recovered, kept evidence of this informal system at work. In his files is the following letter, received in February 1917, when he was working at the medical headquarters, VIII Corps D.A.D.M.S.   .

I want you to try and help me do something for our doctor (one Capt. Andrew, late 87th Fd. Amb. [Field Ambulance]).

Sir Hunter should know him. He did absolute wonders & he is a fine chap but has had enough (after being 3 times buried in ten minutes!) & I want to try and get him to a base hospital. He is very keen on fine surgery & it would of course help him in his practice. I know you are practically the Director so will do what you can. I can vouch for him all right & he is no shirker.

William Tyrrell at that point was also a fine chap who had 'had enough'. His time at the static hospital was extremely uneventful, punctuated by letters of goodwill from men in the Lancashire Fusiliers. 'Sir, all the staff wish you the best of luck and prosperity, and a speedy return to "Olde Ireland",' wrote A. Ellis. Sergeant Bibby wrote to settle a bet they were having on the exact day that Tyrrell had joined the regiment: 'you see, although you have left us some months ago, you are ever in the mind of all, and constantly the subject of conversations, I suppose it is wrong; but I feel sure your name will live long in the old Regiment'. Tyrrell's good friend Captain Spooner, by then with the 5th Seaforth Highlanders, wrote to say 'I will confess with you that I don't mind if I never hear another gun or bullet but at the same time I do not want to be out of it when there is anything on. You I know will understand and probably feel the same.'

This was a common feeling. Ian Whitehead's study of doctors in the First World War gives several examples. The work at the front was stressful, but the work in the base hospitals could be dull. A Dr G. Moore said 'Dreadful life! . . . not much risk of my becoming a base wallah', and Harold Deardon was pleased to escape to 'the more robust and colourful environment of a Field Ambulance' after a few months in 'This backwater, half military, half civilian, and wholly oppressive and enervating'.[12] William's father wrote to him in December to say

I think I can understand your present feelings in consequence of the confining character of your duties where you are at present, but all the same I think you should feel a measure of satisfaction on account of the splendid work you have done for the poor fellows exhausted to your core.

In May 1916 Tyrrell was moved to the No. 1 Motor Ambulance Convoy, a spell which included in June a trip back home to Belfast. In September that year he was moved to a job at headquarters, while waiting to see if he would get a new command posting. HQ was obviously not unduly taxing, as he had time to copy out anglophile poetry in a fair hand – Rupert Brooke and Rudyard Kipling being favourites. He went to a conference on topics such as 'The Diagnosis of Shell Shock' and learned that cases of shell shock were only to be diagnosed at casualty clearing stations if the officer in charge of the man's unit had investigated it. This meeting also covered the problem of rats, with Tyrrell learning that 'rats population depends entirely on available food'.[13] In October 1916 a letter addressed to 'My Dear Billy', from a friend in the ambulance convoy, let slip what was in prospect: 'I want to stay here in case you get your Field Amb as I am very keen still to go up the line again with you.' He did get it: in March 1917, at the rank of lieutenant colonel, Tyrrell was given the command of 76th Field Ambulance, operating close to the action on the front lines.

'Field ambulance' is perhaps a misleading term, as it suggests merely a transport vehicle. Typically, a field ambulance had a total of 238 staff, and medical equipment to cope with approximately a thousand cases. Tyrrell's files contain his own sketch plan for the layout of his main dressing station, which contained 354 beds in all, including a fifteen-bed operating tent and a twenty-bed isolation tent. The 76th Field Ambulance was on the western front, in Flanders, and had its headquarters in Bailleul and an advanced dressing station at Pont St Quentin. In June 1917 the 76th had taken over the front line for the Battle of Messines Ridge. A report by the adjacent Field Ambulance, the

77th, led by Lieutenant Colonel H. B. Kelly, gave the casualty figures that they dealt with on that occasion. Excluding the walking wounded, they processed forty officers and 635 men of the 'Imperial' troops (i.e. UK 2nd Army under General Plumer) , and fifty-two officers and 1,040 men of the 'Colonial' troops (on this occasion, Anzac II Corps).

The battlefield after the capture of Messines Ridge had provided the scene for Ronald Skirth's traumatic exposure to corpses, most importantly the unmarked body of the young boy Hans, on 8 June 1917. William Tyrrell visited the same battle-field, before any signs of organic decomposition were evident. He described for the Southborough Committee these cases of what was then known as 'fatal shell shock', using the then-popular distinction between 'commotional' and 'emotional' shock:

> At Messines Ridge, 7th June 1917, when a mine was blown under the German lines, debris and bodies were evulsed from a depth of 60 feet, depth proved by strata of soil thrown up. I visited it within two hours of the explosion and found dead Germans, three in number, lying unsoiled, unmarked – one with spectacles still on and unbroken – no visible sign or evidence of violence. Eyes and pupils normal, the possibility of gas was excluded. [The shell shock committee pointed out that this did not exclude carbon monoxide poisoning.] This is a classic instance of death from commotional disturbance without visible injury. I have seen other cases, but none so definite or so well proved as this.[14]

After battle came sport. The Divisional Football Competition Final was played at a fete on 9 July in 'commemoration' of the victory at Messines, together with a rugby match, '74th and 75th Brigades versus Rest of Division [i.e. the 25th], captained by Lt.Col. Tyrrell MC (International) and Capt Hughes DSO (Barbarians)'.[15]

By September 1917 Tyrrell's field ambulance was back in
serious action for the Third Battle of Ypres (Passchendaele). His
papers for this period contain evidence of the increasing official
concern about the definition of 'shell shock'. A confidential
memo from the director of all medical services for the 2nd Corps
complained that the orders of June 1917 were 'not thoroughly
understood by Medical Officers' and urged much stronger care
before diagnosing 'shell shock'. The memo sets out a distinction
between two categories. The first group were 'cases which have
received some definite trauma to the nervous system, although
without visible wound, through the effects of British or enemy
weapons'. This group

> should be regarded as battle casualties (Shell Shock 'W') but,
> in order to eliminate any possible error – the cases in question
> must be transferred to a Special Casualty Clearing Station as
> 'N.Y.D.N.' (not yet diagnosed, neurological), to enable the
> Neurologist to personally examine them and to obtain evi-
> dence from the Units concerned bearing on the special
> circumstances under which the condition arose, prior to
> diagnosis.

The second group were cases which 'exhibit symptoms coming
under the general heading of Nervousness, Neurasthenia, Hys-
teria etc while in action'. Case in this group 'must be regarded as
"Sick" and diagnosed in accordance with the nomenclature of
diseases. They were to be transferred to rest stations or evacuated,
depending on the likely treatment time, in the ordinary way.
The main point of the memo was that 'Medical Officers must
bear in mind that all cases diagnosed "Shell Shock (W)" are
classed as battle casualties and entitled to wear a wound badge,
and that every endeavour should be made to limit the gaining of
this dress distinction to really genuine cases.'

The memo did not mention compensation, or qualification
for disability pensions, although these issues must have lain

beneath the policy of differentiating 'W'ounded from 'S'ick. Informal evidence suggests that there was a great deal of latitude in how individuals were treated – Ronald Skirth had one officer tear up a conduct sheet and put him on light duties, just as William Tyrrell was kindly moved back for a rest from the 'turmoil' of the front. Were they 'W' cases, or just 'S'?

The stricter policy on defining 'shell shock' had operational consequences for the medical staff at the front. Tyrrell himself had started diagnosing straightforward cases of 'shell shock' quite early on. In his own list of 'Wounded' for the dreadful month of May 1915, which had included the gas attack, he had listed '2/Lt H Metcalfe Shell Shock 16.5.15' among the gassed and injured. By August 1917 he was being referred queries such as the following message addressed 'to the MO, Menin Road Dressing Station': 'Can you find any symptom of shell-shock, or anything wrong with bearer? So far as I know a shell burst fairly near him, but am not satisfied that he is ill.' (This from H Eaton Hart, Capt, on 3/8/17.)

Tyrrell's copy of the memo on the diagnosis of shell shock, dated 7 August 1917, was located in his papers nestling alongside a memo of 1 July of that year giving instructions on 'Burial of British Soldiers During Heavy Fighting'. This document is based on the premise that 'continued heavy fighting and intense bombardment' may make it impossible to carry out the routine instructions for collecting and burying the dead. It advises placing bodies in shell-holes or trenches and covering them with 'C Solution' (an improvement on quicklime); it also suggests that where bodies are under enemy fire 'it may be possible under cover of darkness to send out a few men with sprayers or improvised sprinklers to reach the bodies, and sprinkle them well with "C" Solution'. This last is a gesture towards the appalling smell of rotting bodies; Guy Nightingale commented on their desperate struggles to lime the bodies in front of their trenches at Gallipoli, as the smell was so unbearable. Military authorities were commonly – as in this memo – rather coy about stating the obvious. Tyrrell himself, when given a list of possible causes of shell shock, in order to prepare his evidence for the post-war Southborough Committee, added 'nauseating sights and smells' to their list in his own handwriting. The final report translated this as 'nauseating environment'.[16]

Disposal of the dead generated a number of disciplinary issues. Clause 1(d) notes sternly that 'cases have occurred of dead being buried in their full equipment and their graves marked by sticking the barrel of their rifles into the earth and writing the man's name on the butt. As the arms and equipment are required, this practice is forbidden.'

Another area of concern, which revealed the army's wondrous ignorance of cultural differences with regard to disposal of the dead, was the graves of men of 'other nationalities and religions'. The memo gives complex instructions about separating bodies of different nationalities, and the rules for establishing separate cemeteries. The document is particularly exercised about the iconography of the Christian cross, whilst seeming not to know that many Indian soldiers would rather not have been buried at all, but cremated: 'Under no circumstances should a cross be erected over an Indian grave. Stakes are provided to take their place. Officers i/c Sections will be responsible for reporting immediately any departure from this order, giving the name of the person who caused the cross to be erected.' Similar strictures were issued about the marking of graves of men 'of the Jewish faith'.

Tyrrell himself continued to command his field ambulance through the slaughter of Third Ypres in autumn 1917, moving on in early 1918 to the battles of the Lys and Lens. By now he had added a DSO to his name. The casualties he had to deal with did not abate. In one field message book, an entry at 1.30 p.m. on 17 April listed the following:

Capt Kennedy	– killed
Sgt Smith	"
Pte Beeching	"
Cpl Smith	w'd will probably die
Pte Ussher	shell shock
Pte Dickson	wded

That was all since his last message at 11 a.m. At 2 p.m. he wrote to encourage a junior officer: 'I cannot express my feelings re our casualties. You must simply "Carry On".' Tyrrell's personal diary entries became terser as the war progressed. On 2 May 1917, exactly two years after the gas attack, he wrote '*Bad night Not up to usual form*'.

In June 1918, personal tragedy was to strike. Two of William's younger brothers were also serving on the western front, both with the Royal Flying Corps. Walter Alexander (known as Alexander), aged only 19 and the eighth of the Tyrrell children, had quite an impressive record of air combat and had already followed in his older brother's footsteps in winning an MC. Among Tyrrell family personal papers are completed reports of his work between 7th April and 6th June, set out on the official Army form 3348 'Combats in the Air', duly signed by Captain (and Flight Commander) W. A. Tyrrell and by Major J. C. Russell, the commanding officer of 32 Squadron. They show that in that particular short period Alexander had brought down eleven enemy aircraft, and on 3rd May he had notched up three of them in one 'offensive patrol'. On that occasion he shot down two triplanes, one over Frelinghien and one over Steenwerke, then forced an Albatross two-seater to land behind allied lines near Poperinghe, enabling the two officer occupants to be taken prisoner by the infantry.

On 9 June he was killed in action near Roye-Montdidier. Although he had been shot in the chest, he managed to get back behind his own lines before crashing, and his grave is in the military plot of Beauvais communal cemetery. Alexander's death was covered in the Belfast newspapers: headlines such as 'Best and Bravest Pilot', 'Wonderful Endurance' and 'Capt. Tyrrell's Last Flight' all paid tribute to this very brave young man and what he had accomplished in the Flying Corps. In December 1919 the War Office posted Alexander's Military Cross to his father in Ireland, with the words 'I am to express to you the Secretary of State's regret that this gallant officer, who gave his life for his Country, did not survive to receive his reward from the hands of His Majesty the King.' William Tyrrell was not able to get there in time for his young brother's funeral, which had taken place by the time he arrived at the squadron. His papers contain a memento of the brother who was fourteen years his junior and to whom he must have been a distant figure – the notebook containing Alexander's technical notes from his time learning gunnery.

Within ten days of Alexander's death a further tragedy was to follow. Billy Tyrrell's favourite brother, John Marcus, was the golden boy of the family. Marcus, as he was always known, was good looking, a brilliant student, charismatic and admired; he was 23 and had transferred from the Royal Irish Fusiliers to the Royal Flying Corps. On 20 June his plane had just taken off near Boulogne when it nosedived from an altitude of only 100 feet, and he was killed. There was no mechanical error found in the plane when inspected afterwards. The cause of his death was never really determined; the suggestion was that he might have fainted at the controls. Perhaps his concentration had been affected by his brother's recent death, or perhaps a moment of fatalistic depression overtook him – it was never clear.

The Tyrrell family were at home at 'The Cairn', Ballyholme, in Bangor, County Down, when they heard the news. According to Mr John Tyrrell they were addressing envelopes, acknowledging letters of condolence on Alexander's death, when the post office telephoned them with a wire from Billy saying 'Marcus killed 20th flying accident'. The family issued a joint announcement of the deaths to many papers, just as after the war their names would be linked on the war memorials of their school (the Royal Belfast Academical Institution) and church (Duncairn Presbyterian). The cause of his death was officially described as 'a flying accident in France' rather than the more noble form of words 'killed in action'.[17] A letter to Mr Tyrrell described the funeral of this very popular young man:

> The funeral was at 2.30pm in the British Cemetery, Boulogne. Billy had arrived early in the morning having come up by car from very far South. Frank Montgomery and myself were the only others from home. A large number of pilots and men attended as well as several lady drivers. There were a very large number of wreaths from squadrons and individuals.

When Marcus died, the press coverage in the papers included an emotional tribute from the headmaster of his old school, the Belfast 'Inst'. He said that Marcus was 'one of those boys whom a master never forgets'. He noted his fine, tall and slender figure, his bright and gay expression, his equally bright and happy temperament, his quick intelligence and his athletic prowess. Marcus was, he said, 'a marked boy' at the school, and that these attributes 'would have made him a conspicuous figure anywhere'. He was, he added, one of those whose presence 'distinctly added to the pleasure and satisfaction of our daily work'.[18] For a schoolboy this was quite an encomium. Marcus was William Tyrrell's favourite brother. From the number of wreaths at the funeral in France, he was also extremely popular with his comrades and colleagues. It is hard to square this golden young man with the manner of his death, ambiguous as to cause and pathetic in nature. An answer of sorts can be found in Marcus's letters home, which reveal an altogether different person: one who was constantly complaining and fearful, particularly to his parents.

Marcus Tyrrell had started off in the Royal Irish Fusiliers. On 4 October 1915, he wrote to his father from the British

Expeditionary Force in France. He welcomed the arrival of new underclothing for his 'very cold carcass' and he noted that the sweets his mother had ordered him from Selfridges had not arrived. 'Luxuries like that seldom come our way,' he wrote, 'they pass through too many hands on the way up to us poor blighters.' He next turned his attention to the progress of the front, about which his father had written to him. 'I wasn't in the "forward movement" that you speak of. I have no regrets about it either, though it is all in a day's work out here . . .' 'You', he added, 'probably know more about it all than I do, as we have received no papers [he means newspapers] for the last few days.' Finally, on this topic, he added that 'anything I could tell you would be struck against the rigid laws of the censor, so I'll not try'. Patently Marcus felt that his father did not appreciate the hardships of life at the front.

There is also in these early letters a hint of a cry for help to his father. Describing the coldness of the trenches, with winter drawing in, he declared that 'there is nothing under the sun so uncomfortable or miserable as turning out of a fairly mouldy dug out to stand to just before dawn. There is no glamour and very little romance at this hour, only a dominating impression of cold.' However, he continued, 'get used to it' was their motto. Turning to another topic he acknowledged that 'the tone of this letter rather reveals my state of liver tonight, and that's not good so don't believe half you read'. This was October 1915 and Marcus was 20. Could it be that his older brother's meteoric success – by then William had been decorated and promoted – had led Marcus to think that the army was more glamorous and romantic than it actually was?

Marcus was then seconded from the Irish Fusiliers to the Royal Flying Corps. In a letter to his mother, dated September 1916, he made it clear that he had found the pressure of the trenches unbearable. He described being under fire, when salvaging a plane that had been shot down: 'I was very frightened when I was up there', he wrote, 'and I know definitely now that

I could not go back to the "line" again'. By this time he was thoroughly ill at ease in the Flying Corps, as he made clear in an extraordinary letter to his father, dated August 1916. The letter is a catalogue of misery, some of it directed towards his parents. 'I looked for a letter from you', he began, 'but nary a scrap did I have from home for six weeks after I left you, altho I think I wrote to mother soon after my return to this wretched country.' Then followed a rather grand account of how successful their operations had been during the past two months, 'tho I says it what shouldn't'. They had been 'adding fame to this very young corps', and they had 'completely asserted our air superiority over the enemy'. This had been done at a cost, the sacrifice of some of our 'best fellows' and 'best machines', but 'no man, no matter how valuable, is irreplaceable' he commented. Marcus went on to conclude that 'we command the air as well as we do the sea', and that much evidence proved that this was understood on the ground in German territory, 'and it is not often that the Hun admits himself second best in anything'.

Marcus's own work at this point was reconnaissance photography. He was the officer in charge of a photographic section which had 'turned out 2,000 prints since last Monday', which meant staying up until daylight during the whole period. The work was behind enemy lines, he said, and it was dangerous. Marcus then told his father in some detail about one particular flight. 'Last Sunday morning when I suppose you were all at church, the aeroplane I was in was absolutely peppered by machine gun and shrapnel bullets.' He said that one bullet passed with an eighth of an inch of his foot, passed upwards between his arm and body and out through the top, and another had hit the windscreen six inches from his head. Marcus appears desperate for his father to appreciate how well they were doing such a dangerous job: 'still', he wrote, 'we got the job done and landed alright'.

Driving home the point about his state of mind, Marcus continued: 'After sixteen months or so now of this sort of work in trenches and here one begins to find a difference in health and nerves. I know I want a long rest but have not the heart to ask for it yet.' Acknowledging that he was longing to be invalided out, he wrote 'I was bitterly disappointed that the bullet missed my foot. I kept the hole well covered with my foot for the rest of the trip, but no more came that way.' He then explained to his father just how badly the odds were stacked against his survival in this type of work. He said that he met very few fellows who had as long a combatant service as he did, so naturally he began to think he was lucky, 'or is it unlucky I sometimes think when feeling utterly depressed and fed up'. He was earning 25/- a day in the Flying Corps, roughly twice his wages in the Fusiliers, and was paying off some debts. Underscoring his expectations, he said 'this is paid to you as long as you are able to fly and of course that is not a score of years; about 8 months out here is the usual time'.

This letter was signed off very formally: 'believe me, your affectionate son, Marcus Tyrrell'. It surely indicates that Marcus was not coping very well with the strain on his nerves. Shortly afterwards, William wrote to his father:

I just got a glimpse of Marcus. He needs his month's leave & more if he can get it. I told him to take things very quietly . . . Marcus knows about sending the Medical Certificate to the War Office, & if the W O ask for a board, I have spoken to the medical people at Victoria & I think everything will go smoothly.

So it is quite clear that by late 1916 William Tyrrell knew his brother was in danger of cracking up. We can only speculate on his state of mind in June 1918. It must have been difficult, throughout his war service, for the boy so admired at home and at school to have failed to live up to the heroic exploits of his older brother William. How did he then feel when Alexander, four years his junior, rapidly overtook him in bravery when he joined the Flying Corps? It must have been difficult being so open to your parents about being afraid, only to have your apparently fearless kid brother decorated and respected. Alexander's death, the 'best and bravest pilot', could well have tipped Marcus's lack of self-esteem into a critical new phase.

Subsequently, poor Mr Tyrrell would have to deal with the estates of both of his sons, a task that brought him into some conflict with the War Office. Marcus had at various points mentioned his debts and money worries. There were problems such as the bespoke clothing he had ordered before he died. Among various items of this kind, the Savile Row firm Sandon & Co. (Breeches Makers, Hunting and Military Tailors) had made Marcus a pair of breeches for £4 19/- which had been posted to him at the front on 10 June and never worn. Whilst they were very sorry indeed to hear of Captain Tyrrell's death, they were not keen to have the breeches returned: 'We find it difficult to bring in finished Uniform for another customer as all our orders are made to measure and in the case of breeches the fit of these has to be so exact.' This position of 28 August was reinforced on 21st September, as 'it is very difficult in our case to ask our customers if they will try on a pair of breeches that have been made for someone else'. They then raised the question 'if your eldest son, Col Tyrrell is at all near in measurements to the late Capt J.M Tyrrell' as a solution to the problem.

Even the Tyrrell family's comprehensive private archive doesn't reveal the upshot of this delicate negotiation. There was, however, one immediate and major consequence of Marcus's death, which had clearly hit the family very hard indeed. The man who had written to Mr Tyrrell about the funeral, Fred Jefferson, addressed both Billy's state of mind, and the anxieties of Mr and Mrs Tyrrell about their third son at the front, when he wrote on 26 June.

> Billy stayed on in Boulogne until Tuesday and I went down on Sunday and spent some hours with him. He came up yesterday to stay with Frank Montgomery where I saw him

last evening. I hope again to see him tonight. I have had a good opportunity to speak to him about coming to a job out of the line and this he has decided to do. Knowing that Billy is not of the nature to ask for such a job I am going to put it privately to the proper authority. (I don't want him to know this, so when writing him don't mention anything about a change.)

The strategy worked remarkably quickly. Alexander and Marcus had died in June, and by the third week of August Billy Tyrrell was taking up his new job as the Deputy Director of Medical Services (DDMS headquarters) at Etaples, where he was to lecture on his RMO and FA work, and generally 'look after the horses'. Suddenly loquacious in his diary entries, he wrote on 18 August 'so after four years of war I become a Base Wallah'. 'First impressions far from rosy'; 'Some stern pioneer work ahead and strange to say even this prospect seems to have stirred me out of my dull despondency of the past few weeks.' He concluded for the day 'I do not relish this dual command − + loss of my identity − It grates after being my own master for so long. It would be utterly impossible with anyone else but Col. Ensor.'

One of the William Tyrrell boxes in the Imperial War Museum's archives does not contain his own documents but those of the two brothers killed on the western front while he was there. Their notebooks and manuals became his property. It was William Tyrrell's handwriting that formally and posthumously designated, on the cover of one set of technical notes, its owner: 'J M Tyrrell, R.Ir.Fusl. & RFC 16 Sqdrn'. Among these pathetic remnants of their short military careers is the Christmas card Marcus sent in December 1917, wishing his older brother 'Good Luck in 1918'.

During his four years of war service William Tyrrell had many terrible experiences, but the two that stand out are his breakdown in the autumn of 1915, and the deaths of his brothers in June 1918. In the course of 1918 he was negotiating his post-war future. He wanted to get a regular commission in the RAMC, but the regulations on drafting civilian doctors were strict and they did not want to set a precedent by giving him a permanent commission. In April 1918 'Willie' wrote to his father for advice. Flying activities were being brought together in the new branch of the services then being formed – the Royal Air Force. William got the impression that he would be able to get a permanent commission in the RAF, on the medical side. Was this a sensible move? What role the deaths of his brothers, both killed in the air, played in his eventual decision we do not know, but the burden of being the oldest son must have been considerable.

Many years later, in May 1939, Group Captain Tyrrell was appointed an 'Honorary Surgeon to the King', occasioning a great flurry of loyalist congratulations from delighted friends and family in Belfast – one card read 'God Save Ireland! God Save the King!' One of the 'Old Contemptibles' regarded it 'an honour to yourself, to your Corps and to our City'. A friend wrote to say 'it is good to know that some Irishmen uphold the honour of the Ould Country when so many are letting it down by their cowardly actions.' (Tyrrell's marriage was clearly waning, romantically speaking, as his wife sent a telegram saying 'Congratulations Do I get anything'.) Jenny Hagan of Fisherwick, Belfast put her finger on the emotional context when she said: 'What a terrible trouble your father and mother passed through when they lost two such promising sons in the Great War, and how happy they would have been today if they had been spared to follow your career and know they had such a worthy son.'

Tyrrell forged a career in the medical side of the RAF, rising to the rank of air vice-marshal. It was as if he worried away, all his professional life, at why he had broken down in 1915, why he had lost control. He became the RAF's expert on fear, on courage, on morale. In 1921 Squadron Leader Tyrrell, Senior Medical Officer at RAF Uxbridge, was asked to give evidence to Lord Southborough's Committee on Shell Shock, meeting at the War Office in April. In February he was sent the terms of reference of the inquiry, in order to prepare his written evidence. Tyrrell's annotations to this document are revealing. In the first place, they show what an authoritarian person he had become by then. By 1921 he had forgotten that his own shell shock required the kindness and tact of those who knew that what he needed was a break from intolerable pressure. The terms of reference of the committee were:

> To consider the different types of hysteria and traumatic neurosis commonly called 'Shell Shock', to collate the expert knowledge derived by the Service Medical Authorities and the medical profession from the experience of the war with a view to recording for future use the ascertained facts as to its origin, nature and remedial treatment, and to advise whether, by military training or education, some scientific method of guarding against its occurrence cannot be devised.

Under this Tyrell wrote:

> Child Welfare
> Development of Character
> "   " Will Power
> Discipline

The accompanying questionnaire rattles through many possible causes of shell shock. Question 15 asks if he has seen shell shock arise from various causes, to which Tyrrell added 'General dissipation'. Asked if shell shock is lessened by home leave, he noted 'Depends how the leave is spent. If quietly it lessens Sh Sh. If Debauchery & dissipation it increases Sh Sh.'

Preparing his evidence, Tyrrell listed what he considered to be the predisposing factors to shell shock. Many of these were standard but some definitely his own, such as 'Mud and Blood', 'Nauseating sights and smells', 'The ever present sense of death'. Finally, and perhaps taken directly from his own experience in

1915, 'leave associated with extravagant and licentious living and Alcohol in excess, succeeded by exposure to intense Stress of Battle'.

Tyrrell's notes continued:

> Training: The recruit 'should be saturated and interested in
>   Tradition
>   Pride of Regiment
>   Esprit de Corps
>   The Fighting Spirit
>   DISCIPLINE'
>   Leadership 'is the most important factor in maintaining
>   morale and reducing Shell Shock'
>   'The Unfit should be *rigidly excluded*'

Of his own case, Tyrrell said

> I have known other cases similar to my own and with satisfactory results on return to the line. I have known many more cases, who came back to the front only to break down again. They had not benefited by their previous experience and had not learnt how to fortify their minds and souls.

But Tyrrell's disciplinary stance was a little at variance with some of his more liberal observations – yes, he had diagnosed cases of insanity which 'in my opinion were due solely to the stress of war' and yes, he knew of the case of a regular non-commissioned officer 'with an excellent pre war character [who] was eventually shot as a persistent deserter'.

William Tyrrell's willingness to give an account of his personal experience of shell shock to the committee was, albeit anonymous, a courageous recognition of forces quite beyond morale and discipline. In later life the authoritarian response became more and more engrained in him. In the RAF he was posted abroad, to Palestine, Iraq, Egypt, India, before returning to seriously 'base wallah' duties in England. He married, not the 'May' of his 1914 diary (who left him during his time in service), but Barbara Colclough of Romsey, Hampshire. The second of their three children, the first boy, was named Marcus Alexander.

In his professional life, Tyrrell became driven by rank and connections. His correspondence files bulge with letters from people congratulating him for his latest promotion, decoration or honour, or thanking him for letters he had sent congratulating them similarly. When the Second World War broke out he was besieged by anyone who had ever met him, trying to get their sons into the RAF. Here is an example of his references, written in 1940 from the RAF's Headquarters, Training Command, in Berkshire:

> McIldowie comes of a good family. He and his older brother were educated at the same school as myself and my brothers, and his older brother served with credit as an officer in the Royal Irish Fusiliers 1914–1918. I can confidently recommend Gunner D W McIldowie for a commission in the Equipment Branch of the Royal Air Force, to which end he can give my name for reference when making his formal application through you. Yours, Air Vice-Marshal . . .

A long footnote to RAF history could be based on Tyrrell's correspondence with young women, never as lucky as Gunner McIldowie. One highly qualified woman doctor was told that the only work the RAF could offer her was in catering or clerical.

Despite his extreme loyalty to the Crown (and delight at being knighted), Tyrrell embarked on a protracted and bitter dispute with the Air Ministry about his pension, when he discovered that the rank at which he would be retired was only that of air commodore. Having married late, he had a young family to put through their education. The ministry did not relent, despite recognizing his contribution to the Second World War effort. In

March 1945 the *Evening News* reported that 'Yet another Very Important Person in the RAF has left the service to take a civil aviation job. Air Vice-Marshal Sir William Tyrrell has just become the director of medical services for British Overseas Airways.'

Captain Lawrence Gameson
Croix de Guerre, Royal Army Medical Corps

When war broke out in 1914 Lawrence Gameson was taking the clinical part of his training. He had studied medicine at Oxford and was working at the London Hospital in Whitechapel. Like other young men of his class and generation, he was keen to join up. Many medical students did try to join up, but were returned to medical school by the authorities. Lawrence Gameson went back to the family home near Walsall, impulsively, to enlist as a private in the local regiment, the South Staffordshire. His father did not agree: 'he recalled my years at Oxford, and one already at the London; said that doctors would be in short supply, that they could not be turned out quickly.' Lawrence went back to the hospital.

He qualified in December 1915, but was not immediately free to do as he wished. First, he had to wait for his medical degrees to be conferred. On the morning of 27 January 1916 he took his degrees in Oxford, and then got the train to London and underwent another kind of medical examination. He was classed A1 fit, and was immediately commissioned as a first lieutenant in the Royal Army Medical Corps. By the end of that same day he had bought himself a uniform. As he put it later, he was 'freed from the, then, considerable odium of wearing civilian clothes'. There would now be another 'infuriating delay' for him. There was a policy in force, supported by the War Office, that newly qualified medical officers should help with staff shortages at home by working another three months in their hospitals.

Only after these reluctant duties at the London were finished could Lawrence Gameson get on with what he considered his real job. On 10 May 1916 he was sent to France, to report to the Deputy Director of Medical Services at the large base at Etaples. That day he began to keep a diary. Waiting at the station in Boulogne 'an ambulance train came in and unloaded, so we had our first glimpse of wounded in France. It was rather a shock. Many men looked exhausted and just about to pass out.'

Dr Gameson was sent first to 24th General Hospital, and was assigned to the 15th Division. By 15 May he was attached to the 45th Field Ambulance, based at Béthune. As we know from William Tyrrell's experience, a field ambulance was a large organization. In his subsequent memoir, Lawrence Gameson described his field ambulance as it trekked from Béthune to the Somme. 'As a spectacle, a Field Ambulance of the period was anything else but inspiriting when on the road. It still had the complement of clumsy horse-drawn ambulances, which moved at a slow walk-march, and whose main functions were to collect stragglers from the infantry columns.' It was, he made clear, completely different from a casualty clearing station. The latter was a tented hospital, staffed by female nurses, and well behind the back areas. 'A field ambulance was very much an affair of the field – both in location and in the crude first-aid work done.'

Lawrence Gameson had a Nonconformist religious back-ground and as soon as he arrived at the Field Ambulance he felt uneasy, socially. There was a lot of drinking in the evening, and he felt 'impossibly out of it' and very lonely. This was to continue, and at the end of May, exactly a month after he had reported for duty in the UK, he was still feeling 'very lonely'. After six weeks of harrowing work at the Somme, his integration with his medical colleagues was no better. On 11 September he recorded 'I am quite dreadfully lonely. I suppose, in a way, I'm a bad mixer, but am not entirely convinced of this. I'm entirely convinced, however, that I do not wish to mix with most of the M.O.'s of the 45th Field Ambulance. And that's flat . . .'

This was to change the very next day. On the night of 11 September the medical officer of 73rd Brigade of the Royal Field Artillery, a Dr Broughton, was killed. Dr Gameson was to report at once to replace him. His feeling was simply 'at last I am with a combatant unit'. On his first day in his new role, he recorded that 'already I feel more at home than ever I did with the Ambulance'. Dr Gameson was put in charge, as medical officer, of the batteries of the 70th and 73rd Brigades of the Royal Field Artillery. He would spend two years with them, before being forced to leave his beloved gunners and move to the Scottish Rifles at the very end of the war. The bulk of his detailed memoir concerns his time with the artillery, but the preceding period, when he was working in a field ambulance at the Somme, contains important information.

The 30 July 1916 was their last day before moving south to the Somme. In the morning there was church parade in an orchard. He noted that the 'Sermon had the obvious theme of laying down your life for a friend. Such exhortations rather annoy me.' The day ended in a reflective mood.

> We move tomorrow. A moth has flown into my candle. It is stuck in the grease. I can give it no help. Antennae, stuck out in front, burnt one by one. The little black-and-white wings outspread. A dark streak shoots through the head and body. One wing gone – pooſh! The other wing – pooſh! Each makes wavering smoke rings. Crackle, crackle, crackle. The grotesque blackened husk is sliding into the liquid wax. The day began with a sermon on death and sacrifice. The holocaust of this little moth comes now at its end. The second sermon is the more provoking of thought.

By 4 August the 45th Field Ambulance had reached the village of Laviéville, near the town of Albert, which was their last stop before going into the line. Gameson, on horseback as officers usually were for these moves, was able to take in what he saw as they arrived.

> The villages are increasingly neglected and dirty as we near the edge of the Somme show proper. Countryside is packed with troops: troops doing P.T., bayonet drill, bombing practice, advancing in open order, jumping in and out of trenches, even playing soccer in the shrivelling sun. Cavalry are exercising. There are acres of camps under canvas, obvious, barely camouflaged. Many prisoners' cages in course of construction. A few occupied.

After they arrived, at 9.30 a.m., he went to look around. He saw what we know to be two of the iconic images of the western front, the broken tower of the church at Albert, legendary for him in 1916; and the blasted trunks of destroyed trees, which appear to have surprised him.

> Have just had my distant initiatory view of the battle-zone . . . In Albert I can see the church one has heard about; can see the gilded figure of the Virgin bent and toppling. A heavy bombardment, clearly visible, is going on far away to the east. It is all happening near some wood. When first I looked at this wood I took it to be the remains of an isolated industrial centre with clusters of chimney stacks still standing. It is a group of branchless tree trunks. It is more like a plantation of telegraph poles. The smoke hides it, blows away then hides it again as I watch. The whole landscape is so outside my ken that I feel I am not seeing France's living face but the nebulous country of dream life or an evil fairyland.

At this point there is a comment in the typescript: '(Approaching the high-flown. It is what I wrote many, many years ago, so it shall stand.)'

At the end of this visual account of the setting and landscape, Gameson added that he had seen a field ambulance coming away from the line to which his was headed – 'they looked exceedingly tired'. Anticipating the conditions ahead, Lawrence had his hair cut short and 'clipped close as a convict's: cool, clean, easy to wash'. From 15 August to 9 September he was part of the team manning the 45th Field Ambulance's advanced dressing station at Contalmaison. This ADS had been set up in the cellars of the shelled chateau of Contalmaison. In the photo albums accompanying his memoir, Gameson included a picture of the chateau, on which he had drawn a blue line to indicate what was still standing in 1916. The line runs along the top of the ground floor.

In 1922, Lawrence Gameson wrote up his memories of this period at Contalmaison. Perhaps oddly, given the dramatic and gruesome nature of the medical work he was doing, what predominated was the sense of unease he felt with his colleagues in the field ambulance. This unease had an element of anxiety, which would recur. He spoke of the 'torture' of being confined with people who jarred and irritated him. There was an element of feeling cut off from the life he had led on the other side of the war. There was also an element of depression, which was to lift as soon as he left the field ambulance.

An advanced dressing station had limited capacities to treat the wounded. There were none of the normal surgical amenities, no antibiotics, no clean clothing for the men. All they could do was dress wounds, splint limbs, adjust tourniquets, give out tea or food, inject anti-tetanus serum and administer morphia, before evacuating the men by ambulance to the rear. If what they could do was severely limited, the quantity of their work was not. In the 1922 account, Gameson gave a detailed description of the throughput of casualties. The flow of work was uncertain, he recorded, 'times of slackness alternating with times of great stress, when the place filled with scores of reeking, bleeding men'. These times of stress 'recurred regularly', 'they went on and on', they worked for hours and hours without a break. The congestion 'beggars description' he wrote; stretchers blocked the passages, the stairs, the floors, the approaches outside. The walking wounded sat on benches or squatted on the floor between the stretchers. Of the conditions in there, Gameson – qualified as a doctor a mere six months before – had this to say:

> Sometimes a man on a stretcher would vomit explosively, spewing over himself and his neighbours. I have seen mounted troops brought in with liquid faeces oozing from the unlaced legs of their breeches. Occasionally a man would gasp and die as he lay on his stretcher. All this was routine; and the waiting crowd looked on perforce. It looked on unconcerned. No one spoke much during these seemingly endless periods of congestion. For the most part, the wounded showed little reaction of elation or tendency to talk and to exchange the customary quips. They waited patiently, while we got on with our work with no needless words. This was done in the poor light of candles and reeking lamps. There was little water, and of course no running water. Dressings and filth accumulated, to be burned outside with the minimum of smoke. The air became rank; worse when gas was about for airways had to be partially blocked. Blood was the general background; dried, drying or wet.

This work at the ADS lasted for about three weeks, after which Lawrence Gameson was given a few days' rest at Fricourt. After Contalmaison, this felt like a 'cosy place', with a mess in a dry cellar lit by daylight. The main job at Fricourt was to provide a link between the RAMC medical staff working near the battle sites and the casualty clearing stations much further away from the line. Gameson was there for three days and then returned to his clinical duties at Contalmaison. He noted that he spent longer there than any other medical officer in the 45th Field Ambulance and that in the few weeks he spent there 'I saw more torn human tissues than one would have thought possible in so short a time.

There was hardly a part of the body I did not see cut or exposed.'
Of this period, Gameson concluded that the work in the cellars
was rudely done, but it was done with the 'singleness of purpose'
of medical men. This quality had, he insisted, 'precious little
nobleness'. It was, he thought, 'a habit arising from rather hard
training in which all wasteful sentimentality is discouraged'.

On 11 September Gameson's unit was relieved by the South
Midlands Field Ambulance and he rode back to Laviéville: 'what
joy to discard the steel helmet, to feel the wind in your hair, to
know again the thrill of unafraid movement'. The next day he
was sent to be a medical officer with the Royal Field Artillery,
where his work was to be very different from the advanced
dressing station. It was also better suited to his temperament.

Gameson's memoir refers at various points to the different
conditions obtaining in the artillery and the infantry. The injuries
he treated at the Somme were largely of the infantry, and he had
an enormous respect for their courage. He wondered how the
infantry 'stick it'. Before going to the Somme he had witnessed a
'show' near the Hohenzollern Redoubt on 8 June. Describing
the affair, he said 'a section of the P[oor] B[loody] I[nfantry]
bursts into action. The noise is entirely outside my experience. I
do not know how the infantry stand its continuity, its repeated
bouts of continuity that is to say, and still say sane.'

Lawrence Gameson hoped his memoir would show how
much the artillery had provided important services to the
infantry, a fact sometimes neglected. On joining the Field
Artillery Gameson was operating further back from the front
line. The artillery's function was to barrage from behind the
enemy lines so that when the infantry went in they met less
opposition. Mostly they were firing over the heads of the infantry
in positions further forward. As a medical officer Gameson had
very great freedom of movement. He was medically responsible
for two brigades and did the rounds himself to check on them.
He would therefore walk a lot, behind the batteries; he had a
'roving commission' and 'wandered at large unchallenged'. In

the lengthy periods between actions Gameson described his activities as 'wandering from battery to battery' passing the time of day with trench mortar talk, writing essays on gas or flies, and corresponding with men he had evacuated.

Gameson kept or copied some of this wartime correspondence and typed letters verbatim into his memoir. In its final preface, he declared that they were 'an indispensable part of this record', throwing precious light on the intimate feelings of families at home. Letters from the families of men who had died were particularly precious to him, with their simple dignity and 'quiet courage of acceptance'. As with William Tyrrell, these correspondences resulted from his role as a military doctor. In Gameson's case, he took it upon himself to bury corpses he found on his travels on the battlefields. One instance is recorded in detail from early October 1916, in the village of Le Sars. Gameson, walking with a colleague, came across the body of a British soldier, not of his division, unburied and decomposing. He took and posted to base the man's identification discs and paybook. He sent to the man's wife his papers and some letters that were on him. One was a letter from his mother, which Gameson found so affecting that he took the trouble to copy it out before sending it on:

Dear Son John
Just a few lines for your birthday. I have just been reading thy letter on to myself. I feel a bit dull today Sunday. I would like to post you a nice present but am getting a pair of stockings knit for thou. John many a cry when I lay down for thou. I am such a bad letter writer. So no more. Short and sweet. God be with us till we meet again.
Love and many kisses,
Mother.

Historians continue to study the letters men sent to their mothers from the front, but the other side of these correspondences has usually not survived. Lawrence Gameson wrote of this one 'Even had I not copied the letter one would have remembered the iambic music of the remarkable "John many a cry when I lay down for thou", read for the first time beside John's pitiful body.'

In John's breast pocket was a photograph of his young daughter, torn by the bullet or shell that had killed him. There was a letter from his wife:

> God knows I have many a weary night and day for I never go to sleep but I see you somewhere or I am talking to you for my mind is so much upset for it is now we know how much we love each other but we will just have to hope for the best and trust you will come safely through it all. May God send you safely through this terrible war safe, from your own dear annie. XXXXXX Goodnight. Love to Daddy from his Bubbles. (I hold her hand, but she wriggles too much)

Gameson and his companion covered John's body with turf and bricks and left him. Lawrence Gameson wondered, as he lay that night to sleep on the damp floor of his cellar, 'what in God's name must the grand total be of ours and the enemy's – if this one man had three generations of women to mourn him'.

Gameson had the opportunity for many more burials in the wake of the Battle of Arras. The 15th Division, in which he was serving, was part of the British Third Army which advanced into German-held territory near Arras in April 1917. The attack had been part of a plan to support the ill-fated French commander, General Nivelle, by diverting German forces northwards from his attack on the Marne. Despite Haig continuing the attack, from April to a final attempt at the beginning of May, the plan was largely unsuccessful. Approximately 150,000 British men were lost in the attempt.

'By the end of April our attack was nearly exhausted,' wrote Gameson, describing the cheerless and treeless slab of land that remained. 'Unburied dead with swollen faces lay about. I set myself to bury them.' His decision to do this is explained in his memoir. It was partly 'a sanitary and aesthetic measure' but not really his business as a medical officer. However he felt that if someone on the spot had time to do it, he should. The dead men were of another division, left behind. So he and a D.V. Tomson (who served with Gameson in the Royal Field Artillery and received an MC and bar) shared the tasks of burying the men, sending the identification discs etc. to brigade office, and writing to their relatives. Gameson kept some of the replies he received, to which he felt he could not adequately respond. He usually had no information other than what was on the body.

Mrs Pickering, widow of Private W.T. Pickering of the 2nd Royal Fusiliers, wrote to ask if her husband had left any message for her when he died. 'It is a great shock for me to bear', she wrote, 'as I am left with 6 little *girls* the baby he as not seen, 1 year old. Please do your best in answering the above, as I should dearly like to know if there was any message for me at any time.' Mrs Grimshaw, widow of Harry, wrote to thank him for his letter. Harry Grimshaw's Sunday school teacher wrote to thank him for breaking the news which the family had not yet received officially, and to wish him 'god Speed in your noble work of healing'. Mr Thomas, father of Herbert, wrote to say one of his sons had been killed at Salonika in 1916 and he had two other boys about to leave for France. His wife had had a stroke. He asked 'in confidence' to know where his son had been killed and for a photo of 'where he lays'. Gameson could not respond, as 'the whole truth would have been needlessly brutal'.

The burial of bodies was only one aspect of Gameson's dealings with death as a doctor attached to a combatant unit. Unlike William Tyrell, who fast became at least as much an officer as a doctor – assuming command on occasion – Lawrence Gameson was never 'soldierly'. He saw himself as having a 'quasi-spectator role' as far as the fighting was concerned. Summing up his position, as of July 1918 when influenza hit his brigade and he had seventy-two men ill with it, he commented that 'as a very non–combatant M.O. I was a *military* nobody in the Brigade, as well I knew. All the same, I used sometimes to feel that such work as I did was regarded as an unimportant matter of course – just a hobby of mine, so to say.'

At times he was able, by virtue of his outsider status in the military, to bend the rules a little. One sergeant got drunk after receiving orders to move forward, in itself an offence against military authority, but Dr Gameson was allowed to quietly put him to bed: 'M.O.s could get away with such things unofficially'.

Gameson had an interest in medical pathology, which even survived all the raw human suffering that he had seen. On one occasion a corpse arrived on a slack day. There was no evidence of the cause of death, usual enough, but Gameson decided to set up a post-mortem. Just as he was about to start, he noticed a tiny dimple in the neck. In this healthy youngster's skin a bullet had entered and the hole had closed over. Dr Gameson the pathologist recalled his 'chagrin' and disappointment that he had to put away the amputation knife and call the post-mortem off. On other occasions, medical curiosity supervened. Walking near the village of Le Sars, he found that the old German trenches were 'crammed' full of dead Germans.

> Some of them had their tongues stuck out and almost severed by their teeth. The eyes of many were sealed with mud. They were mostly quite young men. It was all pretty grim, for they lay on their backs or their bellies in distorted postures of uncomforted agonies. The stink was revolting. I got into one trench to examine them more closely.

Gameson describes one occasion when he was forced into a military role. It was August 1918 and one of his men, having been seriously hit in the spine in a shell burst, had to be got out. He and four stretcher-bearers carried him for a mile and a half, to the aid post, where he was found to be dead. The party refused to return in the dark to their battery, saying that 'nothing would induce them to re-cross that bloody bit of country in the dark'. Gameson gave them a choice: either he would lead them back or he would report them as deserters. Without argument 'the good chaps' went with him, ignorant of Dr Gameson's own struggles with 'windiness', and no more was said about it.

Although Gameson described himself on several occasions as a 'most un-soldierly creature', events proved otherwise. He was promoted within a year to the rank of captain. In August 1918 he heard 'with unaffected surprise' that he had been awarded the *Croix de Guerre*. At the end of the 15th Division's tour of duty with the French, a batch of French decorations had been assigned, including some to the artillery. At the medal ceremony Gameson was the only medical officer, all the other recipients being gunner officers or other ranks. The general who pinned the medal on to him made the double-edged point of saying that the artillery had done him a great honour by 'giving away' one of their medals to an officer who 'is only attached' to them.

Dr Gameson's ambiguous role brought him some very unpleasant tasks. In October 1916 he described in his diary a problem they had encountered in taking over some good German dugouts:

Half way down one of the stairways was a dead German. He had fallen head foremost and was stuck there. On my preliminary examination in the dim light I could see only his field boots. I had come without my torch. Subsequently, on looking closer, I found that his flesh was moving with maggots. More precisely, I noticed that portions of his uniform were heaving up and down where they touched the seething mass below. The smell was pretty awful.

It was the lot of the medical officer to get the short straw.

None of the men would touch him, though troops as a rule are not noticeably fastidious. The job was unanimously voted to me, because it's supposed, quite wrongly, that doctors don't mind. I went down the stairway with a length of telephone wire and lashed it round the poor chap's feet. We hauled him up and dragged him away for some distance. The corpse left behind it a trail of wriggling, sightless maggots, which recalled the trail in a paperchase.

He added that he did not usually bury Germans but on this occasion they used a shell hole as a grave and put up a board with the date.

His attitude to death in the war had been jolted early on. Within days of his first arrival, as orderly officer for the night in the Béthune headquarters of the field ambulance, he had at 1.20 a.m. made an entry in his diary referring to the head wounds from snipers' bullets. They were the saddest, he wrote, with bad prospects and terrible initial wreckage. He noted that 'in the last lot is a surprisingly beautiful youth; long lashes, straight nose, finely finished limbs. He was oozing frothy filth. Would the woman who wished him goodbye now press her lips to the clotted slime about his mouth?' Was that, Lawrence Gameson asked himself, just morbid conjecture? He thought not.

> I wish that more knew more of how men die out here. I've seen good people at home – I've done it myself – gaze almost jauntily down a casualty-list; making the while trite comments of sympathy. Just at the moment I feel that death is not the sole issue. The manner of it should be taken into account.

Gameson was affected by 'the manner' in which dead bodies were disposed of at the front. On 23 May he was at an advanced dressing station at Vermelles, where he attended the burial of a Scottish officer in a small cemetery. 'Bodies for burial', he noted,

> are wrapped in blankets or ground sheets, which hug the human shape and make it look even more dead than it is;

unreasonable, but I know what I mean. A more poignant business burying this kind of package than is burying a coffin, yet somehow more decently simple and less harrowingly beastly.

More 'human parcels' were to follow.

Later that year, at the Somme, Gameson described going through Bazentin Wood. Like High Wood and the other sites of the battles on the Somme from July to September 1916, this wood was full of rotting corpses and had a malign reputation. Lawrence Gameson, a man with an acute literary sensibility, strikingly described this wood in a language that can later be seen inflecting T. S. Eliot's *The Waste Land,* with its image of the sprouting corpse. Eliot's 'That corpse you planted last year in your garden,/Has it begun to sprout?'[1] finds a forerunner in Lawrence Gameson's description of the sprouting fallen trees in Bazentin Wood:

> The wood, a confused mass of living and riven trees, covers a large area. I lost my way in it. A hateful derelict place. I heard no birds, nor any soft scuttle of living creature. Everyone avoids it. I found German corpses and a fragment of German music. The brushwood is growing wildly. The fallen trees are sprouting from their flanks, a blind groping fruitless growth which is horrible. The whole area is horrible; and it preserves the likeness of a living wood. One of the many woods which were bitterly, bloodily contested. Still present there is the lingering air of men's agonies. I was glad to be clear of it. I arrived home very late for lunch.

Gameson's medical orderly, a man named Moir, was killed in the period of preparation for the Battle of Arras in 1917. A year later Moir's replacement, a man of 'lively intelligence' and 'animating cheerfulness' named Arthur Powell, was also killed. Moir was buried on 11 March in Arras Military Cemetery, an unnerving experience. As Lawrence Gameson reported, it was 'a small thing in the telling' but it 'jarred horribly'. It was a new military cemetery, which was not the usual thing of virgin turf. It was a place where there were 'dug graves, parallel rows of them, stretching long lines, empty graves waiting for live young men'. Marching out from the ceremony, some of the men 'lost their footing and fell into the open graves'. Gameson records that 'much laughter accompanied their climbing out'.

As a doctor working at the front, he had to deal with situations that are not often written about. Gameson himself clearly struggled, throughout his life, with the question of whether and how such revolting experiences should be recorded. The nearest William Tyrrell got to this was his repeated mention of 'nauseating sights and smells'. Gameson actually described them in detail, whilst insisting that his record was not for publication. Sqeamish readers may not wish to read this next paragraph.

Perhaps most difficult to read are his descriptions of medical cases where there was necrosis – dead flesh – in living men. His experience of this began at the Somme in the summer of 1916, which he recalled in 1922.

> In one batch of men, I remember, there was a man with a loop of gut sticking out of a gash in his uniform. It was a bayonet wound . . . The loop of gut had been lightly dressed with gauze, beneath which was a wriggling mass of maggots. The man had been lying out wounded, and the flies never missed a chance.

At the advanced dressing station, in the cellars of the chateau of Contalmaison, such sights were commonplace.

> I can recall an unconscious man with a part of a frontal lobe protruding through a hole in his skull. The protruding portion of brain was moving with maggots. When men had to be left out wounded for some time, often their shoulders, buttocks or

whole back were invaded by the creatures in the areas of skin compressed by the weight of their immobilized bodies. One man I saw had been lying out because both his legs were wounded. Prolonged pressure had caused necrosis of the skin over his buttocks and of the superficial portion of muscle beneath it. Maggots had invaded the deeper tissues. I had to pick them out with long forceps. The man was unaware of his condition.

Lawrence Gameson noted that 'maggot invasion was always accompanied by a foul smell, since it flourished only in tissues undergoing some degree of decomposition. As a rule, the victim did not notice the stink, or did not know that it came from his own body . . .'

Not surprisingly perhaps, Dr Gameson developed during this period an impassioned loathing of flies. When he first arrived at Contalmaison, he found flypapers hanging over the table where everyone ate, and struggling and dead flies constantly dropped into their food. He moved the fly papers away from the table. On 13 August he recorded, with evident satisfaction as well as disgust, that

> This evening I killed 14 flies at one swipe with a rolled-up copy of an ancient 'Times'. They are infinitely numerous, leisurely and deliberate in movement and have large sticky feet; neighbourhood is an incubator for them. Eggs are laid in the corpses of Germans and horses, hatching in the rotten semi-liquid flesh. The rest of their lives, for the most part, is an ephemeral gluttonish revel amongst all that is most revolting in this revolting region of putrefaction and decay.

Much later in the war Gameson, a fastidious man who was troubled by the endemic lice at the front, noted the visceral effect on him of the corpses at Bugancy. It was 2 August 1918 and the battle for the chateau and village had taken place on 28 July. The

Seaforth and Gordon Highlanders of the 15th Division had in fact taken the village of Bugancy, but had to retire to their starting position when the supporting French troops failed to get through and left them too exposed. Gameson came across the battlefield as the dead Scottish and German soldiers were beginning to decompose. Walking towards the chateau of Bugancy, Gameson found himself in a field where green wheat was growing.

> Many dead lay hidden in the wheat. I kept stumbling over bodies, for I was looking ahead and not at my feet. Corpses were ripening rapidly in their humidly hot resting place. On that close windless day the evil-sweet stink oozed, so to say, into one's central nervous system and brain. Similar sensory stimuli were by no means unfamiliar, yet the stench of corruption hovering above that cornfield cannot be classified by any standards known to me.

Although Gameson was not easily affected by such smells, he said that on this occasion 'it was several weeks before I could again eat cheese; cheese suggested the other smell'.

Dr Gameson was more aware than most of the anatomical dimensions of what he was witnessing. On 1 April 1917 he noted that he had seen a German pilot killed: his body was 'a bag of bones', and 'had not his uniform held him contained he would have been, as to human shape, pretty well amorphous.' On many occasions Gameson had to engage with decomposing and dismembered corpses, often in the cause of improving the housing of his gunners. In July 1916 he noted that he was trying to improve a particular post by deepening the floor: 'the smell is bad and I keep fishing out bits of German uniform'.

In 1922 Gameson recalled the feeling of depression associated with his early years in service. A note that he made at the dressing station at Contalmaison on the Somme, in 1916, gives an indication of the atmosphere:

Two bodies in room, covered with blankets: head one end, feet the other. It's the repetition which gets on one's nerves. Stiff and still. They obtrude. Seem to fill the place. Can't look away from them. Turned back the blankets and looked at the faces. Covered them up and went to doorway. But, God! The world seems stiff and still today and death is everywhere. Straight in front is a row of ghostly trees; leafless, branchless, no bark, dead. Mist covers the ground and swirls like steam about these stricken trees.

Dismemberment was a routine phenomenon. Visiting a dug-out in May 1918 he commented of the men that 'this morning they'd fished out another decomposing leg from the entrance to their home'. This doctor began soon to feel like a butcher, and the bodies came to look like meat; 1916 again:

> There is a continuous stream of wounded through at all hours. The pips on my tunic cuffs are shiny with polished blood, blood of someone else, of infantry mostly. Although but a middleman, one gets sick of blood's smell and of the endless everlasting procession of red raw human meat passing through our hands.

Gameson's experiences at the Somme exposed him to the treatment of human flesh as 'meat'. In his memoir these grue-some pictures stand out, and differ from his much happier times attached to the artillery. Processing his experiences later, he was ambivalent about what to include in his memoir. He was insistent that the text did not make sense without his original maps. But he wasn't sure of the status of his photograph albums. At first he captioned the images, thinking they could constitute a narrative in their own right. He later decided that they only functioned to illustrate the main text, and tried to delete his earlier 'talky talk' captions. One preoccupation of the albums is the question of 'beastliness', by which he meant corpses. 'I

intentionally avoided pictures of beastliness,' he declared. One
album does, however, carry some French photographs of decomposing bodies, entitled 'Bodies'. They are introduced with
the following comment: 'The rain has washed up lightly buried
bodies and hands stick out. I noticed an officer's leg lying by
itself; a neat boot was on the foot and the leg was covered by a
carefully wound puttee, just as you can see them in the windows
of boot shops.' He continued: 'a purely casual observation made
then as something normal – as it was. The following French
photographs just suggest something of old human remnants,
which were usually (if not too old) swarming with maggots.'
Drawing attention to what could not be shown, he then
announced that 'In the next five volumes there will be no more
photographs of unpleasantness. I cannot stress too strongly that
only a hint has been given of the actual conditions obtaining.'
Interestingly, another album does contain photographs he took
himself of the dead – his horse, 'Bob', and his second horse, both
killed on 11 May 1917, on the outskirts of Arras.

So, what were Lawrence Gameson's experiences of shell shock?
We can look at him first as a doctor treating it, and then as a
man experiencing the conditions that caused it. In May 1917
he encountered a clear case of an inexplicable breakdown. One
evening Gameson happened to be nearby when a shell hit two
men of 71st Brigade who were working in the open, some way
behind the battery. One man fell with a fractured femur and a
'pretty brisk haemorrhage'. The second man was fine, and Dr
Gameson sent him to headquarters, to collect his medical staff
and orderly, while 'I hung on to the bleeding'. This was fine,
and he fixed up the casualty and carried him to the nearest aid
post. The unhurt youth helped with all this, acting quietly and
well, and when the task was done he went quietly back to his
battery.

Later that evening, the youth had broken down. Dr Gameson
knew little about him: he was classed as normal by everyone and

had always come up to scratch. He was used to seeing people hit, to seeing his friends hit, and to being violently disturbed. 'Yet this stray incident broke him.' When the doctor was called late that night, he wrote, 'I found him gibbering'. Later, Gameson recounted:

> The scene is still most vivid to me: the deep, German dug-out, the usual passage running from end to end, the usual tiers of bunks. The place was dimly lit by a few candles. My patient was sitting up in his cramped bunk, leaning forward gripping hard to an upright with both hands. In most of the bunks were men who stirred as they slept. Some woke, but did not complain of the boy's shouting. I spent the better part of the night with him. The conditions were not ideal for such a consultation. I quite completely failed to comfort him. Finally I gave him an injection of morphia, and waited until this rather handsome undoubtedly intelligent child had drowsed in to restless sleep. Early in the morning I took him to the aid post at Les Fossés Farm and he went down the line from there. I did not hear of the boy again.

On another occasion, he was able to do more. In April 1918 'a boy of 17 had suddenly got shell shock'. Gameson immediately noted drily that 'this forbidden term is still current in conversation'. For once in a way, he said, he was able to be of some use, and 'I calmed the poor kid'.

'Shell shock' was indeed officially a problematic category, though widely used in the field. Lawrence Gameson's papers contained, as did William Tyrrell's, discussion of the policies about shell shock being sent down by the military medical authorities. Both doctors' papers contain copies of orders relating to the diagnosis of shell shock, and in particular the need to avoid – in the heat of battle – too hasty a diagnosis of 'Shell Shock (W)', meaning shell shock as a battle wound. Gameson reproduced a letter, sent round in October 1916, from Colonel Bruce Skinner,

Deputy Director of Medical Services for the Third Corps, criticising a report on a man who was wrongly diagnosed as 'SS (W)'. This case had been dealt with by none other than Lieutenant Colonel Myers of the RAMC, the man who first coined the term 'shell shock' in an article in *The Lancet* in 1915. Myers ruled that this man should have been diagnosed 'Shell Shock (S)', or sick rather than wounded, as his condition had largely been caused by 'congenital and acquired nervous instability'. The man in question had twice been rejected by medical boards and 'even while in England proved an unsatisfactory officer owing to his nervousness'. He was, in Myers' view, 'constitutionally unfitted for any form of combatant service'. Myers' basis for making this conclusion was, as Gameson noted at the time, contentious. Myers had declared:

> I have no doubt that the case ought not to be regarded as a battle casualty. He was neither buried nor lifted by a shell. In his own words – 'To tell you honestly it was not *that* (the shell) that made me fall; it was the horrible sight of the arm (blown off by the shell from a neighbouring soldier) flying in front of me.'

Gameson's response to this was extremely sceptical. He rejected the notion that being buried or lifted was the only way a shell could damage a man. Like Tyrrell, he had seen cases of 'fatal shell shock' – men who died with not a mark on them. Gameson attributed this to concussion, which he said 'to my certain knowledge, could play a major part in the after-effects of the near explosion of a shell'. He had seen 'men killed outright by concussion alone without a vestige of evidence of external injury'; he gave a description of one such case, where he examined the man immediately after death. And there were 'lesser degrees of concussion'.

Underlying Gameson's reaction was a conflict within the hierarchy about malingering. He felt that the way medical officers were being encouraged to diagnose shell shock as sickness rather than injury was inevitably tied up with a suspicious approach to the men's health, and a too-easy inference of malingering. Gameson maintained that regimental medical officers were able to deal with it without 'coaching from the rear' as he dismissively described it. This was one of many points where Lawrence Gameson squared up to the authorities trying to regulate his work. At times he was openly contemptuous of their sheer ignorance of the appalling conditions at the front. He also took the view that if a medical officer was doing his job well, malingering was 'remarkably rare'. Explaining this, he merely said that he always took the view that malingering 'was largely influenced by the M.O.'s own approach' and that 'at all times the men knew that they could come to me'.

William Tyrrell believed that the medical officer played an important role in relation to shell shock. As we saw in the previous chapter, Tyrrell received instructions that 'every endeavour should be made to limit' the number of cases diagnosed as shell shock (wounded). Gameson, looking back on this later, was scathing. 'As early as 1916 I had some uneasiness. All this "W" versus "S" stuff seemed a shade tendentious.' Years after the war, and resulting from his involvement as a volunteer in 'helping neglected men to substantiate their claims on the ministry of pensions, and sometimes increase the pittances they were already receiving', he concluded that the distinction between 'W' and 'S' was financial in motive. 'Once a man had been officially labelled "W" – and here is the point – he was in a much better bargaining position than the one marked "S".' Gameson recognized that diagnosis could be difficult: 'we all knew that shell-shock was a highly debatable matter'. But his experiences after the war made him quite cynical. 'For the Ministry of Pensions between the two wars', he wrote in 1958, 'I had the greatest contempt. Of course it had to exercise restraint in its disbursements, yet it was under no obligation automatically to regard almost every claim as suspect; which it did, summoning medical and surgical yes-men to help it wriggle out of its minimal responsibilities.'

A robust position on shell shock, then, from Dr Gameson; how was Lawrence Gameson the man faring? I have referred in passing to his use of the word 'windiness', and to his own struggles with fear that he hid from the men of the other ranks. There is a rich and dramatic thread of information in this vein in Gameson's account, shifting between anxiety and depression until he reached a turning point and moved beyond it to some degree.

Gameson's personal anxiety was apparent to him as soon as he arrived at the front. In his diary of 29 May 1916 he noted: 'the ceaseless slithery sound of shells has somewhat got on my nerves. I am feeling rather anxious and scared tonight. I am very lonely. It is just a month since I reported for duty.' Ten days later, when complaining about the unpredictability of infantry attacks he added a very self-critical comment:

> I have the same maddening feeling of tension as I had when last here. I am profoundly dissatisfied with myself. It boils down, all of it, to my inability not to be anxious. In a multitude of forms, this curse has dogged me since early childhood. I am disgusted to find that I cannot oust it.

During his time at the advanced dressing station on the Somme, passing through the 'raw human meat' he described so terribly, the main feeling he recalled was not horror but anxiety – 'it was almost overwhelming', he said. As we have seen, the dead bodies got on his nerves and depressed him, while exerting a morbid fascination (a common combination in these accounts). Early in 1917, he later acknowledged, he had 'periodic phases of blank depression', more often than not 'unrelated to my immediate surroundings'. It was in the nature of his job that he knew these were common. Gameson wrote several times on the need to disguise his anxieties from his colleagues. Describing one of the local messes, a flimsy shelter a few yards behind the guns, he commented that 'when lunching there one day we were shelled with an 8 inch, and much too close to be healthy. No one minded in the least – which did not go for me had they known – nor was much damage done.'

Another instance of this was noted when he was with a group that was shelled. No one was hurt but it made him angry, an anger he could not show, 'for everyone knows it is a sure sign of having the wind up'. This was 'a chronic condition' for him. One of his commanding officers created a problem by becoming concerned about his welfare when travelling alone visiting the various batteries. The colonel suddenly told Gameson he should take someone with him. Gameson was horrified, as this would interfere with the ways in which he dealt with 'my little daily problem of personal safety'. He believed that

> risks from casual outbursts of shelling were greatly increased if you were with one or more companions. For there was apt to be the useless pretence on the part of each (invariably thinly disguised on the part of me!) that he did not mind and would not be the first to take cover.

Gameson's technique for self-preservation was to listen, and look, with incredible care. He heightened his hearing, honed his response to shells coming over and was constantly looking for the next piece of cover. So ingrained did this habit become that many years later, tramping over countryside that resembled this terrain, in his work as a GP in a rural area, he found that he was doing the same thing – 'apparently pointlessly watching the ground ahead'. These evasive measures only worked because, like Ronald Skirth, he had the freedom to control his own movements. By August 1918, this sensible strategy of self-pre-servation had tipped over into 'a state of anxiety which came near to the pathological'. He could not sleep, he could not explain what was happening. 'Its essence was crude, irrational physical fear', and it dominated his private thoughts. It led him to superstitious behaviour, which he regarded as 'morbid'; for instance, in always using one entrance to the HQ dugout and not the other. He managed, 'still desperately in private', to shrug it off and lift these 'vain taboos' but he continued to be held by a 'ghastly tension'.

It was at this time of feeling 'emotionally under the weather', combined with a patch of very heavy shelling, that the incident of evacuating the man with the broken spine had occurred. After he had led the mutinous stretcher-bearers back to their battery, Gameson set off for HQ. On the way a shell burst right behind him, pitching him forward. It was dark, he tripped on some barbed wire and went head first into a shell hole. His tin hat bashed on to his nose; he got a mouthful of earth. Still possessed by the state of acute anxiety he had been suffering from, he did not see any funny side to it. His morale 'reached its lowest point ever', he said, 'I crouched there in a blue funk'.

His state then could be likened to Tyrrell's, when he had crouched in a dugout in a state of terror. But Gameson was not next to be buried alive, as Tyrell had been – precipitating his breakdown. For Gameson, 'these moments of humiliation' were a turning point. He could not account for the change, 'mental, spiritual or both', that came over him. His morale 'soared'. He liked the juxtaposition of events: 'so recently had I been shepherding recalcitrant sheep, while now I shivered alone in a shell hole'. He spat out the earth and pushed on. A trivial incident, and only of interest to himself. In point of fact, he recalled, 'it was a milestone', and one that is of more general interest. This turning point sets the scene for the rest of Gameson's memoir. We have so far heard relatively little about his private life. At one point we hear that he didn't go to prostitutes 'for one thing, because I am engaged'; at another, that 'most of my leaves were unrefreshing'. It was not until May 1919 that he would break off this unsatisfactory engagement.

Meanwhile, less than a month after the shell-hole funk, he had met Learoyd. They struck up an extraordinary friendship and one which Lawrence Gameson was hesitant to write about, even many years later, 'for I continue to regard this ground as inviolable'. It was October 1918 and Gameson was stationed near Mazingarbe. The war was ending. Learoyd was very young – he was called 'the Babe' – and he wanted action. He was a liaison officer in the Black Watch regiment, who were just forward of Gameson's artillery brigade. Gameson's memoir gives an indication of what the boy found in the medical officer: one of his letters was delivered to him at HQ. 'It bore neither name nor address, but simply had "The Faith Healer" emblazoned in purple pencil across the front of a buff army envelope.' The boy, an excellent horseman and a rider to hounds at home, was offering to take Gameson, 'the brigade's leading dud on a horse', out for a ride to teach him how to tackle some low jumps. 'We had a delightful afternoon.'

Lieutenant Learoyd was impatient. He had come out to France when the fighting was almost over and was 'crazily keen to distinguish himself, since soldiering was his profession'. One day he invited Gameson over to the Black Watch battalion headquarters, introduced him to the colonel and then proposed an outing. He would 'stroll out in front' to try to ascertain the enemy's position at first hand: 'Doc dear, do come with me!' He brushed aside Gameson's objections to the plan's 'lunacy', and said he was going anyway. Surprisingly, for a man who had been so anxious, Gameson decided to go with him.

They set out, soon meeting a small Black Watch patrol. The sergeant in charge said the wood 500 yards away was held by the enemy, whereas Learoyd thought that the Seaforths had a post there. The patrol went off, Learoyd managing to borrow a revolver from one of the men. They continued walking towards the wood, crossed three belts of barbed wire, making no attempt to conceal themselves, when they suddenly came upon some Germans. Gameson knew Learoyd would 'advance on a hidden machine gun, brandishing his pinched revolver, with the fatuous hope of getting the Huns to surrender'. He took charge himself, forced Learoyd instantly to the ground, got them both flat, and ordered him to wriggle back to the wire. The Germans opened up with machine gun fire but they were not hit, though Learoyd got a bullet hole through the seat of his breeches. They managed to get into a hole between two of the belts of barbed wire. There, temporarily safe, they reviewed the situation.

Gameson, comparing the situation with his blue funk a month before, felt some satisfaction in his present predicament. He had prevented 'the Babe' from getting killed and they might get out. They swapped doggerel poetry and cod verse quotations until another machine gun started up. At this, Gameson decided they had to get out. He insisted they toss a coin for who should go first, won and slithered to the next belt. Calling for Learoyd to join him, at last 'the tiresome child' wriggled into view. They escaped eventually, and got through the third belt of wire on their stomachs, after which 'we got up and ran like blazes'. When safe, Gameson took a photograph of 'my treasured lunatic, quivering happily'.

The next day, they found that the sergeant whom they had met had been killed by the machine gun on their flank. This cast a different light on their adventure and brought them both into some disfavour. On reflection, Gameson said the whole episode was characteristic of Learoyd in its folly. He had nearly got them both killed. They had no business to be where they were; they were ignorant of the techniques needed and were unarmed. The incident showed how much Gameson had changed since the turning point, the milestone marking his low morale. He had needlessly exposed himself to more danger. He had exposed himself emotionally too, for his feelings for 'my Babe' were deep: 'outside the ties of blood my attachment to him was unique'.

Gameson reproduced the last letter he received from Learoyd. A regular army officer, he was stationed in India and had just been recommended for a Military Cross. He asked his friend

Gameson 'Are you married yet?', adding 'You know I'm sure you could make whoever you were in love with very happy.' Soon after that 1920 letter, Learoyd died. Gameson had a period of years, 'longer than his whole span', to look at Learoyd's letters and reflect upon the 'vivid boy, whom I held so very dear, in whom I was so absorbed'. During that period he looked upon the letters, and 'tangible things which closely bear on him', with an unchanging 'tenderness' and 'reverence'.

Shortly after the escapade with Learoyd, Gameson had one of his periodic contretemps with the authorities. In this instance there was an outbreak of flu, and he was treating the cases himself when the orders had been to evacuate them. Accused of arrogance, he was sent off, forced to leave his beloved gunners, to be medical officer with the 10th Scottish Rifles at Petit-Rumes. It was 30 October 1918: 'this date was to be for ever the vilest spot in the calendar: ringed, so to say, with black for mourning and with red for anger'.

The attachment to the Scottish Rifles, at the very end of the war, would last only six months. To his great surprise, the officer who had been in charge of the 45th Field Ambulance in 1916, Lieutenant Colonel Frank Worthington, sent for him again. Gameson was to join him at the 5th Army Headquarters; he reached Lille in April 1919, and spent five uneventful months working there.

It was only in 1955 that he decided to write up an account of what happened next. Gameson's long and detailed war narrative, accompanied by precise map references and a series of descriptive photographs, now turns into a love story. A reserved man, he had said little of his personal life, although he had referred to an engagement in very lukewarm terms. In May 1919 he finally broke it off, deciding to do so by letter, as he had twice previously done so in person and been persuaded 'to eat my words'. The third attempt was successful and his decision was accepted; he was a free man. He described the arrival of the Women's Legion Ambulance Drivers in Lille with a laconic observation that was typical of him. Ostensibly, he said, their function was to replace troops and hasten the process of demobilization. In fact, their real purpose was to supply bored men awaiting demobilization with 'girls from home as companions'. One such was a young Women's Legion ambulance driver called Helen James. They met on 21 September 1919; by 2 November they were engaged to be married. Gameson described his feelings with great charm. On one occasion Miss James was acting as a chauffeur to him and the vehicle broke down. Under orders not to leave her ambulance unattended, and with night falling, their problem was solved when she was picked up by a Women's Legion car. Gameson (and his batman) spent the night guarding the A16 ambulance. Sunrise came and 'at last came the girl who had gone, came the girl I was waiting for . . . I did not realise, even then,' he wrote, 'that all my life I had waited for her.'

Lawrence Gameson suffered from what he called 'idiotic hesitancy'. He could not propose to Helen; he was hiding his feelings in 'a ridiculous pose of indifference'. In short, he said, 'I had become virtually dumb'. On 2 November he managed it; on the 3rd he went to town on his motorbike and bought a ring. Exactly one year after the day that had been 'the vilest spot in the calendar', his life had changed completely. Two years hence the same day 'was to stand out in my life for such signal joy': this was the birth of their first child, named Felix. Lawrence and Helen were married on 26 January 1921. After Felix came two more children, Maureen and Hugh. The Gamesons evidently had a long and very happy marriage: he died in 1972 and she, on the day of her wedding anniversary, in 1979. They were, according to their daughter in law, in love with each other for the whole of their lives. 'They were very close,' said Felix Gameson; he doted on her, and he hated her going out.

Lawrence Gameson held several posts as a doctor, working in general practice, in hospitals and, during the Second World War, in military psychiatry. A man with a considerable interest in literature, he spent many years on a project translating Baudelaire's *Les Fleurs du mal* into English verse. He also wrote poetry himself, and was a keen gardener. At the family home in Bishop's Castle, Shropshire, where he had his own medical practice from 1926 to 1933, he even used his wartime knowledge to construct a dugout at the bottom of the garden for the children to play in. Could it be that he had survived his gruesome war experiences without undue psychological damage? It certainly seemed that he had, until I met his son Felix and discovered that for much of the 1930s his father had been an alcoholic. By 1933, when the family left Bishop's Castle, his alcoholism was established; he spent the rest of that decade struggling with it until he had a serious accident in 1940. He had been lying on the floor of his surgery, drunk, with his head against an electric fire. He was hospitalized for the damage to his head, and stopped drinking completely. Gameson had prided himself during the war on his abstinence with regard to alcohol. It caught up with him later, adversely affecting the entire decade of his children's teenage years. He was in and out of hospital, drying out, moving from one practice to the next; his drinking made it difficult to have visitors in the house. In 1957 he and Helen finally settled down, buying a house in the village of Curry Rivel, near Langport in Somerset, where they lived until he died.

Afterword

These five men all survived the war, but to different degrees. Willis Brown and Douglas Darling are the saddest of these lives: Willis Brown survived, but not at all well, and Douglas Darling survived, but not for long. Willis Brown suffered physical illnesses for years, was not able to process his experiences emotionally and, until his second marriage, could not manage independently of his parents. Detailed knowledge of his life stems largely from a family memoir, written in the 1960s by his sister Margaret, in which she tried to explain to his son why his father had been so inadequate. In her view, it was his experiences at Gallipoli in 1915 – where he was exposed to some of the very worst conditions of the war, was shell-shocked and invalided out with enteric fever – that had ruined his life and marred his capacity to be a father.

Douglas Darling was also exposed to considerable stress in the war. The battle for Vimy Ridge in 1917 included the use of machine guns to an unprecedented extent, and Darling was in charge of a barrage. In the months after the battle he thought he was shell-shocked, and became increasingly unable to face being under fire. Darling, a brave and conscientious man, wanted to return to the front line, but was kept on at the machine gun school at Camiens rather than returned to his combat unit. In the course of his period in action, from late 1916 until he was demobilized in 1919, Darling wrote frequently and at length to the woman he married in early 1918; although he was careful about the military details, he was forthcoming about the state of his nerves, describing his loss of confidence in some detail. He died six years after the war, and his family were in no doubt that his early death was caused by the effects of shell shock.

These two men were damaged, both physically and mentally, by their experiences in the war. But they were not 'mental cases', in the sense that Wilfred Owen used that term in his poem 'Mental Cases'. Owen's description of 'men whose minds the Dead have ravished' emphasizes the place of bodily destruction, in the causes of mental breakdown in the war: 'wading sloughs of flesh these helpless wander'. Owen did not live to see the recovery of some of the 'mental cases' of the war, and in his poem he describes the 'human squander' as 'rucked too thick for these men's extrication'.[1] Willis Brown and Douglas Darling were among the men who did extricate themselves, after the war, from apparently less serious forms of psychological damage.

Ronald Skirth's experience allows us to consider the view that religious faith can protect individuals from psychological disintegration in very stressful circumstances. His 'mystical' episode in the church at San Martino preceded an amnesiac breakdown from which he recovered as a pacifist. His pact with the Almighty, and his relationship with Ella, kept him going through the last year of the war. His strategy was unusual to say the least, and an audacious evasion of the spirit of military law in the interests of pacifism. At times what he describes is tantamount to sabotaging the work of the artillery from the inside, which he found (not surprisingly) empowering. Skirth's experiences were described in detail in his unpublished autobiography, a project that he worked on for many years, including during his retirement. Skirth's autobiography includes some contemporary items, such as postcards from him kept by Ella, but is mainly a much-revised narrative written with some hindsight. At times it is too self-conscious, too much a fictionalizing of an experience, to be of use to any discipline-bound historian. But it reveals, in its sequential textual revisions, a fascinating processing of, and working on, the experiences of a young man.

William Tyrrell is a complex figure. At first he comes across, in the huge collection of his papers that has survived, as a very likeable young man; by the end of his life he has become obsessional, embittered and authoritarian. He suffered a bout of shell shock, in late 1915, which he appears to have mastered, as he mastered his war experiences more generally. The deaths of two of his younger brothers, in June 1918, affected him greatly, not least in that he himself came out of the front line and into a less dangerous role. More troubling than the heroic death of Alexander was the ambiguous accident that killed the fragile Marcus. But did William see just how troubling it was? The letter in which Marcus told his father he was trying to get a flesh wound, to get out, reads now like a desperate cry for help. It has an inscription on it in William's handwriting: 'a very interesting letter from Marcus to father'. By the time of the committee of inquiry into shell shock, William Tyrrell had formed the view that 'The unfit should be rigidly excluded. They are better left at home, they fill the hospitals, clog movement, and later on swell the pension lists.'[2] William's father had told him he thought 'Marcus was unfit to fly' on the day he died: was William thinking of his brother when he made his submission?

Lawrence Gameson was, it seems, the man who survived most humanely these inhumane experiences. It is significant that the form his subsequent period of pathology took was alcoholism, as throughout the war he was so restrained. When he arrived in France he felt that his Nonconformist (Temperance) background made him ill-suited for socializing in the mess. By the end of the war he had graduated to one glass of light beer of an evening, after which he would escort home others who had got 'quietly oiled'. An alcoholic breakdown for nearly a decade in the 1930s was damaging to his career as a doctor and to the teenage years of his children. It is a tribute to his strength of mind, and the strength of his marriage, that he was able to recover in 1940.

These men survived against rather slim odds. The 'presumed dead' telegram to Willis Brown's parents had already been dictated by the time he was found alive. Douglas Darling could easily have been among the 11,000 Canadians whose names are carved into the soaring memorial at Vimy Ridge. Ronald Skirth and William Tyrrell could have been with the dead of the Ypres salient listed on the Menin Gate and at Tyne Cot cemetery, and Lawrence Gameson's name could well have been on the Thiepval memorial of the Somme, or on several further north. Had these men died, they would have been commemorated, as individuals, by name, on one of the memorials on the western front or at Gallipoli.

At this distance, some ninety years from the end of the war in 1918, how might we think about the differences between those who died and those who survived? The presumption (on the Western Front anyway) for a long time was that the deaths, and therefore their commemoration, were the most important thing. Hence the need to register the fate of these men publicly; to name them one by one, to draw attention to these individual lives cut short. The emphasis on the endless actual names of the dead men resulted in what Thomas Laqueur has called 'commemorative hyper-nominalism'.[3] But for many years now, the meaning of the war has increasingly been seen not just in terms of casualty lists, tombstones and war memorials, but in terms of its wider human consequences. The experiences of the bereaved widows and parents, the orphaned children, the nurses, the conscientious objectors and pacifists, have all been brought to the fore. In the story of 'John', with the letters from the man's mother and wife, Lawrence Gameson spoke eloquently of the three generations of women mourning one man. It was very unusual, though, for a military doctor to transcribe such letters before returning them to the next of kin. The archives mostly contain the letters of the men, not those of their families.

Taking the example of my own family, compare the accounts of one man who died and his mother. In the family
record book, an imposing daybook, the entries are more or less
restricted to births, marriages and deaths, with a few notes of
baptisms and the like. But in the case of Eric, killed in the war,
details have been included such as the date he joined up (27th
August 1914), not just the day but the *time* he first went to
France (2.30, 18 March 1915), when he came back wounded,
when he returned to France. Also logged, for him, are religious
milestones such as exactly when he first acted as an altar server
in church. The combination, especially perhaps as he was born
on 25 December (1889), has the effect of retrospectively
constructing his death in a sacrificial register. By some miracle
of archiving, there also survives a little personal notebook kept
by his mother as a diary during the periods that she was sent, in
the summer, by her doctor to take the waters at Harrogate,
from 1917 to 1920. Mostly it consists of pathetically recorded
details: the times of booking hot baths, the number of sulphur
drinks taken, the length of walks in the Valley Gardens. Once,
on one of her many visits to church, she sees an altar boy who
'brought my boy back to me'. More frequently, the war
intrudes in terms of seeing a plane, hearing the bombing on
the coast, mistaking thunder for guns, and we find her 'praying
that my darlings at home and away may be kept safe from all
danger'. And so she might, poor woman: as well as having her
youngest child long since 'missing, believed killed', she had
another son in the army, one in the navy, and a daughter in the
Voluntary Aid Detachment.

I mention these sources to underline the fact that these war
stories do not derive from individual or cultural memory. My late
mother (born in 1918) could remember her grandmother's grief,
but there can be no personal memory attached to these family
documents for someone of my age looking at them now. But
there is affect and these stories are very moving. The stories of the
men in *Casualty Figures* are affecting in a way that is not to do

with memory, and only about family history for the immediate descendants of these men. They speak to us not because of nostalgia, or sentimentality, or a supposed 'cultural memory', but because they illuminate the personal and human consequences of war.

Notes

Preface

1 Siegfried Sassoon, *Sherston's Progress* (London: Faber & Faber, 1936), p. 88.
2 Norman Fenton, *Shell Shock and Its Aftermath* (St. Louis: Mosby, 1926).
3 Raymond Williams, *Marxism and Literature* (London: Oxford University Press, 1977), Chapter 9, 'Structures of Feeling', (defined p. 132).

Introduction

1 Michael Moynihan, *A Place Called Armageddon: Letters from the Great War* (Newton Abbott: David and Charles, 1975), Chapter 4, 'Gallipoli Survivor'.
2 *The Wells Journal*, Friday, April 26 1935 [front page], 'Funeral of Major G. W. Nightingale' and *The Central Somerset Gazette*, Friday, May 3 1935 [page 2] 'Major Nightingale Buried at Wedmore'.
3 R. C. Sherriff, *Journey's End*. Set in March 1918 and first performed in 1928. Currently in print as a Penguin Modern Classic.
4 Sean Keating, quoted in *William Orpen: Politics, Sex and Death*, ed. Robert Upstone (London: Imperial War Museum and Philip Wilson, 2005), p. 37.
5 Pat Barker, *Regeneration* (1991), The Eye in the Door (1993), *The Ghost Road* (1995), published as *The Regeneration Trilogy* (London: Viking, 1996). *Regeneration*, film by Gillies MacKinnon (1997).
6 C. S. Myers, 'A Contribution to the Study of Shell Shock: being an account of three cases of loss of memory, vision, smell and taste,

admitted into the Duchess of Westminster's War Hospital, Le Touquet', *The Lancet*, February 1915 (I), pp. 316–20.

7 Lord Southborough, Report of the War Office Committee of Inquiry into Shell Shock (London: HMSO, 1922). [Hereafter referred to as Southborough Report.] p. 32.

8 Southborough Report, p. 190.

9 Virginia Woolf, *Mrs Dalloway* (London: Penguin, 1992), pp. 94–5.

10 W. Owen, 'Insensibility' (1917–1918), in *The Poems of Wilfred Owen*, ed. Jon Stallworthy (London: Chatto, 1990), pp. 122–3.

11 Virginia Woolf, *The Years* (London: Penguin, 1971), p. 72.

12 *Belfast Evening Telegraph*, 18 June 1918.

13 A. P. Herbert, *The Secret Battle* (London: Methuen, 1919), p. 105.

14 Sir Alan Herbert, CH, *A.P.H.: His Life and Times* (London: Heinemann, 1970), p. 45.

15 Sir William Orpen , KBE, RA, *An Onlooker in France, 1917–1919*, revised edition (London: Williams and Norgate, 1924), p. 20.

16 Quoted in Bruce Arnold, *Orpen: Mirror to an Age* (London: Cape, 1981), p. 316.

17 Paul Nash, *Outline: An Autobiography and Other Writings* (London: Faber & Faber, 1949), pp. 110–11.

18 Ibid., pp. 194–5.

19 Paul Nash Collection, Tate Library and Archive, London.

20 Ibid.

21 *The Times*, 6 September 1916.

22 *The Times*, 2 September 1916.

23 *The Times*, 4 September 1916.

24 Imperial War Museum, First World War Artists Archive, C. R. W. Nevinson, letters from Department of Information, 4 and 6 December 1917.

25 Imperial War Museum, First World War Artists Archive, William Orpen, 1918 file.

26 Southborough Report, p. 33.

27 Reginald Pound, *A.P. Herbert: A Biography* (London: Michael Joseph, 1976), p. 53.

28 Leonard Sellers, *For God's Sake Shoot Straight: The Story of the Court Martial and Execution of Temporary Sub-Lieutenant Edwin Leopold Arthur Dyett* (London: Leo Cooper, 1995), p. 146.

29 Herbert, *The Secret Battle*, pp. 106–7.

30 The Commonwealth War Graves Commission Archives in Maidenhead, UK, contain many files on Kipling's work with them.

The archive catalogue, compiled by Alex King, was published in 1977 and can be consulted at the British Library.

31 Rudyard Kipling, 'The Gardener' in *War Stories and Poems* (Oxford: Oxford World's Classics, 1999), pp. 310–20.

Lieutenant John Willis Brown

1 Peter Liddle, *Men of Gallipoli: The Dardanelles and Gallipoli Experience, August 1914 to January 1916* (London: Allen Lane 1976), p. 190.
2 A. P. Herbert, 'Helles Hotel' in *The Bomber Gipsy* (London and New York: Methuen, 1919).

Captain Douglas Darling

1 G. W. L. Nicholson, *Canadian Expeditionary Force 1914–1919: The Official History of the Canadian Expeditionary Force in the First World War* (Ottawa: Queen's Printer, 1962), p. 253.
2 Library and Archives Canada website: 'The Battle of Vimy Ridge, April 9–12, 1917'. http://www.collectionscanada.ca.

Bombardier Ronald Skirth

1 W. Owen, 'Strange Meeting' (1918) in *The Poems of Wilfred Owen*, op.cit., pp. 125–6.
2 General Sir Martin Farndale, KCB, *History of the Royal Regiment of Artillery: The Forgotten Fronts and the Home Base, 1914–18* (London: The Royal Artillery Institution, 1988), p. 177.
3 Bruna Bianchi, 'Psychiatrists, Soldiers, and Officers in Italy During the Great War' in *Traumatic Pasts: History, Psychiatry, and Trauma in the Modern Age, 1870–1930*, eds, Mark Micale and Paul Lerner (Cambridge: Cambridge University Press, 2001), pp. 222–52.
4 Ibid., p. 240.
5 Farndale, *The Forgotten Fronts*, p. 184.

Air Vice-Marshal Sir William Tyrrell

1 William Tyrrell archive, Imperial War Museum. [See Sources and Further Reading.]

2 J. C. Latter, *The History of the Lancashire Fusiliers, 1914–1918*, Vol. 1 (Aldershot: Gale and Polden, 1949).
3 Ibid., p. 25.
4 William Tyrrell archive.
5 Latter, *Lancashire Fusiliers*, pp. 39–40.
6 Ibid., p. 40.
7 Ibid., p. 41.
8 William Tyrrell archive.
9 Ibid.
10 Ibid.
11 Southborough Report, pp. 88–91.
12 I. Whitehead, *Doctors in the Great War* (London: Leo Cooper, 1999), p. 210.
13 William Tyrrell archive.
14 Southborough Report, p. 33.
15 William Tyrrell archive.
16 Southborough Report, p. 31.
17 William Tyrrell archive.
18 Ibid.

Captain Lawrence Gameson

1 T. S. Eliot, 'The Waste Land' (1922) in *The Waste Land and Other Poems* (London: Faber & Faber, 1940), pp. 25–44.

Afterword

1 W. Owen, 'Mental Cases' (1918) in *The Poems of Wilfred Owen*, op.cit., pp. 146–7.
2 Southborough Report, p. 33.
3 Thomas Laqueur, 'Memory and Naming in the Great War' in *Commemorations: The Politics of National Identity*, ed. John R Gillis (Princeton: Princeton University Press, 1994).

Sources and further reading

Sources

The five men whose stories are told here – Willis Brown, Douglas Darling, Ronald Skirth, William Tyrrell and Lawrence Gameson – have papers deposited in the Documents Department of the Imperial War Museum. These collections can be consulted by appointment. I also read many other private papers there, including those of Guy Nightingale and Ebenezer Fairbrother, both of whom are quoted in the Introduction. Some of the supporting material used in the book, such as the first-hand accounts of the RNDE in Gallipoli, material on the organization of the Royal Army Medical Corps, and the regimental histories quoted, was also obtained via the reading room of the IWM, which supplies both documents and printed books.

In researching the work of the war artists I consulted the files in the Art Department of the Imperial War Museum, the Royal Academy of Art archives, and the archives at the Tate. Work on the doctors, psychologists and others involved in treating shell shock was complemented by archive work at the Wellcome Library, the Bart's Hospital Archive, the Cambridge University Manuscript Collection and University College London Archives.

Further Reading

There is an extensive historical literature on shell shock and the following are suggestions for getting a sense of the field:

P. Barham, *Forgotten Lunatics of the Great War*, New Haven and London, Yale University Press, 2004.
P. Leese, *Shell Shock: Traumatic Neurosis and the British Soldiers of the First World War*, Basingstoke, Palgrave, 2002.
B. Shephard, *A War of Nerves: Soldiers and Psychiatrists, 1914–1994*, London, Cape, 2000.

First World War studies generally tend to be inflected with either a historical or a literary disciplinary emphasis, the latter having its founding text in Paul Fussell's 1975 classic, *The Great War and Modern Memory* (London: Oxford University Press). Scholars using a literary methodology to open up less traditional questions include:

M. Higonnet (ed.), *Nurses at the Front: Writing the Wounds of the Great War*, Boston, Northeastern University Press, 2001.
S. Das, *Touch and Intimacy in First World War Literature*, Cambridge, Cambridge University Press, 2005.

Specific books relevant to the Army medical side of this project, and on which I have drawn in the text, include:

I. Whitehead, *Doctors in the Great War*, London, Leo Cooper, 1919.
F. S. Brereton, *The Great War and the RAMC*, London, Constable, 1919.
T. B. Nicholls, *Organization, Strategy and Tactics of the Army Medical Services in War*, London, Bailliere, Tindall and Cox, 1937.

Acknowledgements

I am grateful to the Leverhulme Trust for awarding me a twelve-month fellowship in 2003, which enabled me to undertake the research for the book, and to Queen Mary, University of London, for sabbatical leave in 2005, which enabled me to complete it.

The bulk of the research was done on private papers held in the Documents Department of the Imperial War Museum in London: many thanks to Anthony Richards and Rod Suddaby for their unfailing helpfulness. The museum's Department of Printed Books lets its lucky readers browse the open shelves, whilst also offering expert advice, for which I am grateful. The Art Department at the IWM provided archive material on the war artists: particular thanks to Michael Moody for taking me down to the vaults, early on, to show me Orpen's wonderful watercoloured drawing 'A Death Among the Wounded in the Snow' (reproduced here in black and white).

Research on the war artists has also benefited from my being able to consult material in the archives of the Royal Academy of Art, and the archives held at the Tate, to whom I am also grateful. On the medical side, I would like to acknowledge the assistance of the Bart's Hospital archive, the Wellcome Library, the University College (London) Special Collections and the Cambridge University Manuscripts Collection.

In addition to materials publicly available, I also benefited enormously from personal information from relatives of some of the men whose stories are told here. Meeting and talking to them was always helpful, often emotional, and sometimes revelatory. I would particularly like to thank Ms Jean Skirth for letting me read material not deposited at the War Museum. Mr and Mrs Felix Gameson provided fascinating information that materially altered the interpretation I had previously made of Lawrence Gameson's memoir. William Tyrrell's daughter, Mrs Philippa Lloyd, cast helpful light on her father's life, as did the candid views of his son, Marcus Alexander Tyrrell. The copious Tyrrell archive at the IWM included little about the deaths of Alexander and Marcus Tyrrell in 1918, which were an important factor in William Tyrrell's trajectory, and the present Marcus Tyrrell has now donated this new material to the archive. In addition, I am grateful to the copyright holders of all the papers in the Imperial War Museum's documents collections, for permission for material to be quoted.

This research was done in the working context of the School of English and Drama at Queen Mary — it has a unique engagement between the literary and the historical, from which I have learned a great deal. Thanks to QM colleagues past and present: Markman Ellis, Paul Hamilton, Lisa Jardine, Tracey Loughran, Philip Ogden, Daniel Pick, Rachel Potter, Chris Reid and Morag Shiach. Much of the writing was done in the country, away from the charms of the department, and thanks are due to Dilys and Howard Thomas, and to Jean Radford and Luke Hodgkin (descendant of George Hodgkin, 1880–1918). At Verso, my thanks to Tom Penn, Tania Palmieri and Sophie Skarbek-Borowska. Finally, many thanks indeed to those friends and relatives who have listened at some length to the progress of these stories, and given much useful advice: Catherine Hall, Mary McIntosh, Ruthie Petrie, Peter Stallybrass and, especially, Duncan Barrett (*agent extraordinaire*).

Index

A. P. H. : His Life and Times
(autobiography by A. P.
Herbert) 18–19
Abbeville 74, 75
affect 157
Albert (town) 124, 125
alcoholism viii, 5, 6, 7, 8, 9, 151,
155–6
amentia 81–2
amnesia 2, 3, 9, 17, 26, 44, 67,
74–75, 78, 83, 88–89, 154
anxiety 63, 126, 144–6, 147
Anzac beach, Gallipoli 43
archives 10, 31, 59, 115, 116,
156, 157
Armistice 64, 73, 84, 90
Army Service Corps 9
Arras (battle of) 60, 130, 135, 140
Arras military cemetery 135
Asiago Plateau (battle of) 85–86,
88
Asiatic Annie (gun) 43–4
Astico river 85–86
Bailleul 104
'balloonatics' 16–17

Barker, Pat ix, 10
Battle of the Somme, The (1916
film) 22
Baudelaire 150–51
Bazentin Wood 135
Beaucourt 29
Beauvais communal cemetery
109
Béthune 27, 123, 134
Bianchi, Bruna 81– 83
Black Watch, The (regiment) 147
Black, C. S. 38
Blomfield, Reginald 31
Boulogne 110, 115, 123; British
Cemetery 111
breakdowns (emotional, mental)
1, 3, 4, 12, 13, 17, 19, 26, 27,
29, 44, 67, 68, 76, 78, 83, 101,
116, 140, 146, 154, 155
British Expeditionary Force
(BEF) 75, 92, 111–12
British Overseas Airways 121
British Third Army 130
Brooke, Rupert 104
Brown family – [Father] 40, 46–

7, 49, 50; [Mother] 40, 47–8, 49, 50; Anne [daughter] 47, 48, 50, 51; David [son] 2, 48, 50, 51; Enid [second wife] 50; Ethel [first wife] 47, 48, 49, 50; [Ethel's father] 47–8; Helen [sister-in-law] 49; Malcolm [brother] 49; Margaret [sister] 2, 39, 40–1, 45–6, 48, 49, 50–1, 153; Michael [son] 50; 'Mops' 49–50

Brown, Willis 1–2, 15, 17, 28, 31, 34–52, 153, 154, 156

Bugancy 137, 138; chateau 138

Bulwark, HMS 5

burial alive 4, 14, 101, 146

Burlington House 45

Byng, General Sir Julian H. G. 54, 57

Byron, George 72

C Solution 107

Cambridge University 46–7

Camiens Machine Gun School 61, 63, 153

Canadian forces 27–8, 54; machine gun corps 2, 54, 59, 60; Overseas Expeditionary Force 2, 54, 58

Cape Helles cemetery 32

Caporetto (battle of) 75, 81

casualty lists 1, 134, 156

Catholicism 76–7

Central Somerset Gazette 7

Charing Cross Hospital, London 39

churches 3, 7, 64, 67, 76, 77, 83, 84, 86, 87, 94, 111, 125, 154

Churchill, Winston 1, 28, 30, 35

Coldstream Guards 27

Coleman, Elizabeth 7–8

Collingwood battalion 44

'commemorative hyper-nominalism' 156

compensation 4–5, 11, 106

Conscientious Objectors 3, 85, 156

Contalmaison Advanced Dressing Station 126, 127, 137, 138

corpses 1– 3, 6, 9, 17– 19, 22–33, 36–39, 41–42, 45, 52, 69–71, 73–4, 90, 99, 105, 107–08, 129–30, 132–35, 137–40, 144

courts martial 29, 30, 74

cowardice vii, 28

cultural differences 108

Dardanelles Campaign *see* Gallipoli

Darling family – Bee [wife] 55, 61, 62, 63, 64; Bee [daughter] 64; George [son] 5, 64, 65; W. M. [brother] 54

Darling, Douglas 2–3, 5, 8, 15, 17, 27–8, 32, 53–65, 153–4, 156

Dead Germans in a Trench (painting by Orpen) 23

Deal Naval Hospital 34

Dean of Durham 22

Deardon, Harold 103

decomposition 17, 19, 29, 74, 99, 105, 107, 135, 137, 138

depression viii, 17, 61, 81, 82, 110, 114, 126, 138, 144

desertion vii, 28, 73, 81, 119, 133
discipline (military) vii, 4, 16, 17, 29, 67, 78, 81, 82, 93, 118, 119
dismemberment 139
Divisional Football Competition 105
Douaumont ossuary 22
dressing stations 57, 102, 104, 107, 126, 128, 134, 136, 138, 144
Duncairn Presbytarian Church 111
duty 2, 17, 63, 83, 84–5
Dyett, Edwin 28–9
dysentery 2, 28, 30, 36, 37, 38
Eliot, T.S. 135
emotional and commotional shock 25, 105
Etaples 116, 123
Evening News 121
execution 28, 29, 73
exhaustion viii, 46, 47, 82, 104, 123
Fairbrother, Ebenezer 27
fatal shell shock 11, 24–6, 71–2, 105, 142
fear 1, 2, 4, 14, 17, 18, 93, 101, 117, 144, 145–6
field ambulances 4, 102, 103, 104, 106, 108, 123, 124, 126, 127, 128, 134, 149; 45th Field Ambulance 123, 124, 126, 127, 149; 76th Field Ambulance 104; 77th Field Ambulance 104–5
flies 29, 30, 37, 41, 136, 137
Fontanella First Aid Post 88
Frelinghien 109

Freud, Sigmund 10
Fricourt 127
Gallipoli 1, 2, 6, 15, 18, 19, 22, 28, 29, 30, 31, 34–45, 51–2, 107, 153, 156
Gameson family – Helen [wife] 4, 150–51; [father] 122; Felix [son] 150, 151; Maureen [daughter] 150; Hugh [son] 150
Gameson, Lawrence 4–5, 11, 12, 15, 16, 17, 25–6, 28, 32, 122–51, 155–6
'Gardener, The' (story by Rudyard Kipling) 32
gas 25, 63, 81, 95–7, 105, 107, 109, 127, 129
General Hospital, 24th 123
George V, King 22, 39
Ghandi 88
Golden Treasury 68
Gordon Highlanders 138
graves 27, 28, 30–32, 43, 108, 109, 134, 136
guilt 8, 29, 30, 72, 74, 82, 83, 87
Haig, General 72, 132
'Helles Hotel' (poem by A. P. Herbert) 42
Herbert, A. P. 18–19, 28–9, 30, 42
High Wood 32, 135
Highland Light Infantry 38
Hood battalion 44
Hohenzollern Redoubt 128
home leave 4, 13, 14, 56, 57, 64, 65, 67, 82, 83, 84, 89, 90, 99, 100, 114, 118, 119, 146

horses 4, 19, 26, 75, 95, 101, 123, 125, 137, 140, 147
hypnosis 80, 82
hysterical illnesses viii, 10, 15, 106, 118
Imperial War Graves Commission 30–1
Imperial War Museum viii, ix, 3, 5, 14, 37, 65, 68, 116
influenza 131, 149
'Insensibility' (poem by Wilfred Owen) 12
Irish Guards 30, 31
Iser Canal 97
Italian psychiatric authorities 81
Jefferson, Fred 111, 115–6
John Bull (newspaper) 29
Journal of the Royal Army Medical Corps 94–5
Journey's End (play by R. C. Sherriff) 8
Keating, Sean 9
Keats, John 68
Kelly, Colonel H. B. 105
King's Own Scottish Borderers 18
Kipling, John 30–1
Kipling, Rudyard 30–32, 104
Krithia, Second (battle of) 43
Krithia, Third (battle of) 44
Lancashire Fusilliers 3, 13, 43, 72, 92, 93, 95, 98, 99, 102
Lancet, The 11, 142
Laquer, Thomas 156
Latter, J. C. 98
Laviéville 124, 128
Layton family [author's maternal]

– Charles William Gates, died December 1915 ['one great–uncle's name . . . on the Menin gate'] 32; Eric William Layton, died September 1916 ['another on the memorial at the Somme'] 32; his niece Mary Layton 32; his mother Lizzie May Layton 32–33, 157; his brother in the army Reginald Layton 157; his brother in the navy Cyril W T Layton 157; his sister in the Voluntary Aid Detachment Geraldine Layton 157; his niece (the author's mother) Helen May Layton 157
Le Sars 129, 132
Learoyd [friend of Gameson] 147–9
Lee, Major Arthur 23
Leed, Eric 17
Leicester Galleries, London 23
Lens (battle of) 108
Les Fleurs du Mal (Baudelaire) 151
Les Fossés Farm Aid Post 141
lice 137
Liddle, Peter 38
Lille 149
'Lines Written Among the Euganean Hills, North Italy' (Shelley) 68
Lloyd George, David 30
London Hospital, Whitechapel 122, 123
London Underground 42
Loos, Battle of 27, 31

Lys (battle of) 108
Mad Woman of Douai, The
(painting by Orpen) 19
madness 19, 22, 27, 73, 101
maggots 28, 29, 133, 134, 136,
137, 140
malingering vii, 11, 81, 142,
143
Manchester territorials 41, 45
Marne 130
Maudsley Hospital 27
Mazingarbe 147
Mediterranean Expeditionary
Force 35
memorials ix, 27, 31, 32, 99, 111,
136
memory ix, 158
Men of Gallipoli (book by Peter
Liddle) 38
Menin Gate 31, 32, 156
Menin Road Dressing Station
107
'Mental Cases' (poem by Wilfred
Owen) 154
mental / psychological damage
viii, ix, 1, 12, 51, 151, 154
Messines ridge (battle of) 3, 17,
24, 25, 66, 68–72, 104–5
missing bodies 31–33
Montegrotto spa 79, 80
Montgomery, Frank 111, 115
Moore, Dr G. 103
morale vii, 4, 22, 63, 81, 93, 102,
117, 119, 146, 148
Morgan, Major 36
Morto Bay 42
Moynihan, Michael 7

Mrs Dalloway (novel by Virginia
Woolf) 12–13
Mudros Harbour 42
Myers, C. S. 11, 142
N.Y.D.N (Not Yet Diagnosed,
Neurological) 106
Nash, Margaret (wife of Paul) 20,
21
Nash, Paul 19–21, 23, 24
nausea 1, 17, 18, 29, 30, 69, 74,
108, 118, 136
Navy reservists 35
necrosis 4, 28, 136
Nelson battalion 44
nervous strain 2, 15, 28, 56, 58,
60, 61, 62–3, 64, 106, 114,
138, 139, 142, 144, 154
nervous system 25, 106, 138
Netley Hospital 10
neurasthenia 10, 15, 79, 80,
106
Nevinson, C. R. W. 23
Nicholson, G. W. L. 58
Nightingale, Guy 6–8, 18, 107
nightmares 30, 101
Nivelle, General 130
No 1 Motor Ambulance Convoy
104
North Italian Front 3, 16, 66, 67,
75–91
observation balloons 16–17
Onlooker in France, An (book by
William Orpen) 19
Oratory (London) 64
Orpen, William 9, 19, 23, 24
Owen, Wilfred 12, 72, 154
Oxford University 30, 122

pacifism 3, 52, 66, 72, 84, 154, 156
Palestine 46
Palmer, Samuel 21
Paschendaele *see* Ypres, Third (battle of)
passive resistance 78, 86, 88
Paths of Glory, The (painting by Nevinson) 23
pensions vii, 5, 10, 11, 66, 91, 106, 120, 143, 155
Petit-Rumes 149
Piave, Battle of the 90
Pilckem 97
Pilkington [in Skirth's account] 67
Place Called Armageddon, A (book) 7
Plumer, General 105
Pont St Quentin 104
Poperinghe 109
Portland Naval Hospital 45
post–traumatic stress vii
Poven 99
Prue Copse, Middle Wood 25
psoriasis 15, 78, 80
Queens University, Belfast 92
RAF Uxbridge 117
rats 104
reason / sanity / insanity 3, 5, 13, 19, 26, 44, 73, 91, 119, 128, 135
Regeneration (1997 film) 11
Regeneration (novel trilogy by Pat Barker) 10, 11
religion 3, 76, 78, 79–80, 82, 88, 89, 90, 108, 123, 154, 156, 157
Rhine Army of Occupation 46

Rhys Davids, *Lt* (portrait by Orpen) 23
Rivers, W. H. R. 11
Rowley, Captain W. J. [Tyrrell's adjutant] 97
Royal Fusiliers 131
Royal Academy, London 5, 6
Royal Air Force (RAF) 4, 93, 95, 110, 117, 119, 120, 121
Royal Air Force Medical Service 12
Royal Army Medical Corps (RAMC) 4, 81, 94, 102, 117, 122, 127, 142
Royal Belfast Academical Institution 111
Royal Field Artillery (RFA) 2, 3, 15, 25, 45, 52, 124, 128
Royal Flying Corps 4, 14, 109, 110, 112, 114
Royal Garrison Artillery 67
Royal Irish Fusiliers 14, 110, 111, 112, 113, 120
Royal Marine Brigade 35
Royal Munster Fusiliers 6
Royal Naval Division 1–2, 28, 29, 34, 35, 36–7
Royal Naval Division Engineers (RNDE) 34–5, 42, 43, 44, 45
Roye-Montdidier 109
rugby 92, 94, 105
Russell, Major J.C. 109
Salonika 46, 131
San Martino 3, 76–8, 83, 90, 154
Sandon & Co. (Breeches Makers,

Hunting and Military Tailors) 115
Sassoon, Siegfried vii
Schio Hospital for Neurasthenics 79, 80, 82
Scottish Rifles 124, 149
Seaforth Highlanders 102, 138, 147
Seale Hayne Hospital 10
Secret Battle, The (novel by A. P. Herbert) 18–19, 28, 29, 30
Sellers, Leonard 29
Shell Shock vii–ix, 1–5, 8–18, 24–5, 28, 62, 65, 67, 73, 78, 80, 88–9, 93, 99–100, 102, 104–8, 117–19, 140–44, 153–55
Shell Shock and Its Aftermath [1926 study by Norman Fenton of shell-shocked American soldiers] vi, 9–10
Shell Shock (W) and Shell Shock (S) 11, 106, 107, 141–2, 143
Shelley, Percy 68
Sherriff, R. C. 8
Sherston's Progress (book by Siegfried Sassoon) vii
Sims, Charles 5–6, 8; son Alan 6; son John 5
Skinner, Colonel Bruce 141
Skirth, Ronald 3, 15, 16, 17, 24, 25, 26, 32, 66–91, 105, 107, 145, 154–5, 156
Skirth family – Ella [wife] 3, 24, 71, 75, 79, 80, 83–4, 90, 154; Jean [daughter] 78, 90
Slade Art School 20
sleep therapy 80, 82

smells 1, 18, 19, 27, 30, 39, 73, 107, 108, 118, 132, 133, 136, 138
Snow, Major [Skirth's CO] 73–5, 88–9
Somali, HMS 42
Somme dressing station 144
Somme , The (battle of) 4, 19, 25, 32, 57, 123–25, 128, 136, 138, 139, 144, 156
South Midlands Field Ambulance 128
South Staffordshire Regiment 122
South Wales Borderers Territorials 53
Southborough Committee of Inquiry into Shell Shock 12, 14, 17–18, 25, 93, 99–100, 105, 108, 117–18
Spooner, Captain 98, 99, 103
Spresiano 90
Static Hospital No. 4 102
Steenwerke 109
Stewart, Captain 54, 56, 60, 61, 63
Stringer, Bishop of Yukon 60
Suez Canal 46
suicide 4–9
Territorial Army 47, 52
The Waste Land (poem by T.S. Eliot) 135
Thiepval memorial 32, 156
Times, The (newspaper) 22
Tomson, D.V. 131
Tonks, Henry [friend of Orpen] 19

trauma 7, 8, 29, 81, 82, 102, 105, 106, 118,
trees (damaged and destroyed) 19, 20, 21, 125, 135, 139
Treviso Hospital 82
Trotman's Road 44
Tyne Cot cemetery 156
Tyrrell family – [Father] 92–3, 103–4, 110, 111–12, 113, 115, 117, 155; [Mother] 112–13, 115; Alexander 4, 14, 15, 109, 110, 114, 115, 116, 155; Marcus 4, 14, 15, 110, 111–16, 155; Barbara [wife] 117; 'May' [girlfriend] 120; Marcus [son] 120; Philippa [daughter] 165
Tyrrell, William 3–4, 8, 11, 12, 13, 14, 15, 17–18, 25, 32, 72, 92–121, 123, 129, 131, 136, 141, 142, 143, 146, 155, 156
unfit for service 119, 142, 155
unknown warrior 32–33
Veneto, the 76
Verdun 22
Vermelles Dressing Station 134
Verona 75
Vicenza 75; hospital 78, 88
Vimy Ridge (battle of) 2, 17, 27, 32, 54, 56–61, 65, 69, 153; memorial 27, 32, 156
Vlamertinghe 96
Void (painting by Nash) 21
Voluntary Aid Detachment 157

W Beach 42
Walmer Castle 43
Walmer RNDE camp, Kent 35
war artists 19–24
War Neuroses [film made at Netley and Seale Hayne hospitals] 10
War Office 23, 35, 110, 114, 115, 117, 122
war poets ix, 12, 72, 154
Wells Gazette 7
Western Front, visual appearance of 5–6, 9, 19, 21, 24 [and see trees]
Westminster Abbey 32
Whitehead, Ian 103
Williams, Raymond ix
'windiness' 4, 133, 144, 145
Women's Legion Ambulance Drivers 149–50
Woolf, Leonard 13; brother Cecil 13; brother Philip 13
Woolf, Virginia 12, 13
Worthington, Frank 149
Yealland, Lewis 11
Years, The (novel by Virginia Woolf) 13
Ypres, First (battle of) 27, 32
Ypres, Second (battle of) 95, 97 [gas attack], 100
Ypres, Third (battle of) 3, 17, 26, 32, 64, 66, 72–5, 88, 89, 106, 108
Zillibeke 27